Dragon versus E

Dragon versus Eagle

The Chinese Economy and U.S.-China Relations

Wei-Chiao Huang
Huizhong Zhou
Editors

2012

W.E. Upjohn Institute for Employment Research
Kalamazoo, Michigan

Library of Congress Cataloging-in-Publication Data

Dragon versus Eagle : the Chinese economy and U.S.-China relations / Wei-Chiao
Huang, Huizhong Zhou, editors.
   pages cm
   Includes bibliographical references and index.
   ISBN 978-0-88099-403-3 (pbk. : alk. paper) — ISBN 0-88099-403-7 (pbk. : alk.
paper) — ISBN 978-0-88099-404-0 (hardcover : alk. paper) — ISBN 0-88099-404-5
(hardcover : alk. paper)
   1. Economic development—China. 2. China—Economic policy. 3. China—
Foreign economic relations—United States. 4. United States—Foreign economic
relations—China. I. Huang, Wei-Chiao. II. Zhou, Huizong, 1947-
   HC427.95.D73 2012
   330.951—dc23
                              2012045886

The facts presented in this study and the observations and viewpoints expressed are
the sole responsibility of the authors. They do not necessarily represent positions of
the W.E. Upjohn Institute for Employment Research.

Cover design by Alcorn Publication Design.
Index prepared by Diane Worden.
Printed in the United States of America.
Printed on recycled paper.

Contents

Acknowledgments

The papers in this book were presented during the 47th annual Werner Sichel Economics Lecture Series organized by the Department of Economics at Western Michigan University (WMU) during the academic year 2010–2011. The series is made possible through the financial support and cosponsorship from the W.E. Upjohn Institute for Employment Research and WMU's newly founded Timothy Light Center for Chinese Studies. We are grateful to our colleagues in the Department of Economics at WMU for their cooperation and assistance during our effort in organizing and directing the lecture series. We are also grateful to the production staff of the W.E. Upjohn Institute for Employment Research, particularly Kevin Hollenbeck, Richard Wyrwa, and Allison Hewitt Colosky, for the superb editorial services rendered in the publication of this volume. We are, of course, most grateful to the six esteemed speakers of the series and authors of the papers; without their cooperation the publication of this volume would not have been possible.

1
Introduction

Wei-Chiao Huang and Huizhong Zhou
Western Michigan University

It is a market economy, it is a nonmarket economy. It is capitalist, it is communist. It is a superpower, it is a developing country. It is a world factory, it is a global polluter. It is a nation of innovation, it is a nation of imitation. Its people are thriving, its people are suffering. It brings wealth to us, it takes jobs away from us. Such are the varied perceptions of a nation called China. In spite of frequent and ever-growing exchanges between the United States and China in business, culture, tourism, and almost all other aspects of social activities, in spite of overwhelming media coverage about China and extensive research, to many Americans, China is still a dragon behind a mist curtain.

Diverse, even diametrically opposed views of China reflect China's multiple, complicated, and ever-changing facets on the one side, and lack of understanding and historical and ideological biases on the other. In addition, like any bilateral and global trade, China's rise and its relations with the United States will inevitably create winners and losers, although the gains outweigh the losses for both China and the United States. For example, while large amounts of imports have made abundant goods and services available to Americans at affordable prices for the last two decades, they have replaced some domestic manufacturing businesses and jobs. The different experiences or prospects of the consequences of U.S.-China relations will certainly affect the perceptions and views of China.

The 2010–2011 Werner Sichel Economics Lecture Series, "Dragon versus Eagle: The Chinese Economy and U.S.-China Economic Relations," invited six prominent scholars to deliver lectures on China's economic development and power, the driving forces of its growth, its trade relations with the United States, and the impacts on the U.S. economy. We are pleased to present the edited version of their lectures in this collection.

The primary concern from the U.S. perspective is, unsurprisingly, U.S.-China relations, especially as they relate to economics. The economic relationship between the United States and China is crucially important for both countries because they depend on each other; they are integrated. The United States relies on China for cheap consumer products and for financing the U.S. debt, while China relies on the United States for export markets, technology, and foreign direct investment. China is the second-largest trading partner of the United States, with a total volume of imports and exports of $457 billion in 2010. The long-term trend in the U.S. trade deficit remains a key policy concern for the United States and its global trading partners. The overall U.S. merchandise trade deficit increased to $915.6 billion in 2006. China's share in the merchandise trade deficit raised particular concern. The deficit with China increased rapidly and reached $235 billion in 2006 and $273 billion in 2010. In addition, China is the largest creditor of the United States, holding $1.12 trillion in U.S. Treasury bills, according to the U.S. Federal Reserve.

Robert B. Koopman, in his chapter titled "U.S.-China Economic Relations and Value Chains in Global Production Networks," points out that while much attention has been paid to the increasing merchandise trade imbalance with China, it is useful to consider this trade relationship in a broader context. He brings our attention to the changes in the composition of the United States with a number of its main trading partners. In 1989, imports from the United States' largest Asian partners (Japan, China, Korea, Taiwan, Malaysia, and Singapore) accounted for 43.9 percent of U.S. non-oil imports. By 2007, the same share had dropped slightly to 41.5 percent. During this period, the U.S. share of imports from many of its other Asian partners declined. Between 1989 and 2007, the combined share of Japan, Korea, Taiwan, Malaysia, Singapore, and other Asian countries in U.S. non-oil imports dropped from 41.1 percent to 20.9 percent. Thus, much of China's increasing share of U.S. non-oil imports came at the expense of other Asian countries, particularly Japan, which dropped from 22 percent to 8.9 percent of U.S. non-oil imports during the same period.

To fully understand what was happening in global trade flows, Koopman's research delves further into value-added components of trade. By focusing on gross values of exports and imports, traditional trade statistics give us a distorted picture of trade imbalances between countries. Value-added trade statistics help reveal the real economic impacts of global trade on domestic and foreign countries. The value-added approach demonstrates that many countries may add value to a particular good or service in a global supply chain, and that attributing the entire export value to the last exporting country can provide a misleading picture of the sources of value in trade.

China is often the final assembler in a large number of global supply chains, and it uses components from many other countries to produce its exports. Since processing exports have accounted for more than 50 percent of China's exports every year since 1996, imported intermediate inputs used in production for exports are contributed by other countries, including the United States. Accounting for value added, the contribution of China to the U.S. trade deficit differs substantially from what the traditional trade data suggest. The U.S.-China trade deficit on a value-added basis is considerably smaller (by about 40 percent in 2004) than on the commonly reported basis of official gross trade. By contrast, Japan exports parts and components to countries throughout Asia; many of these components are eventually assembled into final products and exported to the United States. Thus, the U.S.-Japan trade balance on a value-added basis is larger than the comparable gross trade deficit. The U.S. value-added trade deficits with other major trading partners (Canada, Mexico, and the EU-15) differ by smaller amounts from their corresponding gross trade deficits.

Koopman also identifies three major factors that contribute to the growing trade imbalance between the two countries and to China's more recently growing trade surplus with the world. The first factor is China's extensive use of policy instruments to encourage its rapid economic development and transition from a centrally planned economy to a market-driven economy. These policies include, among others, incentives for foreign investment and export performance, the establishment of special economic zones and substantial infrastructure investment, and a managed exchange rate. A second explanation focuses on more macroeconomic factors, suggesting that significant imbalance in the U.S. savings and investment rates, combined with relatively rapid consumption-led economic growth in the United States compared to other developed countries, have led to an increased current account and merchandise trade imbalance. A third factor has been the rapid growth in fragmented global production processes, as businesses take advantage of declining costs in information and communications and international logistics to distribute pieces of their production chain based on lowest cost sources. Although fragmentation of global production has developed independently of China's policy environment and is a widespread phenomenon, a large part of China's growth in exports to the United States has been in processing trade carried out by the foreign-invested enterprises, which have been encouraged by and benefited from China's "imports for exports" policies.

What is the size of the Chinese economy relative to the United States? Is it an economic superpower or a developing country? What have been the driving forces behind the unprecedented growth for more than a decade? In Chapter 3, "China's Economy from an American's Perspective," Gene H. Chang offers a balanced view of the Chinese economy and its potential problems.

The true size of China's economy has been a subject of some debate. Using the official exchange rate and the figures reported by the State Statistics Bureau of China, China's GDP in 2010 was $5.7 trillion, ranking second in the world. This is about one-third of the U.S. GDP, which is $14.6 trillion. It is slightly larger than third-ranked Japan, which generated $5.4 trillion in GDP.

However, with a population of 1.3 billion people, China is still poor. Its per capita GDP is only about one-tenth of that in the United States, ranked the 94th in the world. Its per capita consumption of energy, for example, is about 15 percent of the United States. In addition, economic development in China has been quite uneven, with the coastal regions much more developed than the inland.

To put the development of the Chinese economy in perspective, Chang compares the sector composition in China with other countries. Economic theory and history indicate that in the preindustrial period, agriculture contributes the most value added to a country's GDP. In the middle stage of industrialization, manufacturing and industry add the most value. Finally, in a developed economy, the service sector adds the most value to GDP. China's service sector is relatively small, adding value of $2.563 billion, which is about 22 percent of that of the U.S. service sector. In the industry sector, the value added is $2.751 dollars, which is 85 percent of the output of the U.S. industry. While agriculture in China accounts for less than 10 percent of GDP, it contributes a total of $564 billion, more than three times as much as that of the United States.

No one would doubt that China has experienced a remarkable growth at an annual rate of around 10 percent for three decades, lifting hundreds of millions out of poverty. As a result, the standing of the Chinese economy in the world moves upward quickly. In 2000, China's economy was behind most large industrial economies. Then China passed the U.K., France, Germany, and finally Japan in 2010, becoming the second-largest economy in the world. Based on certain assumptions, it is projected that China would overtake the United States to become the largest economy by 2020.

What explains the rapid and sustained economic growth of China for three decades? Many have suggested reasons ranging from the Chinese culture and system to purely timing and luck, but none is uncontroversial. Chang focuses on some obvious economic reasons, namely, the high rate of capital formation supported by the high rate of savings, and the political system, where governments have strong influences over the economy and control the banks.

In terms of fixed capital investment and saving as percentages of GDP, China is ranked near the top of the world. China spends 45.6 percent of its GDP on fixed capital formation. The country has been enthusiastically pouring money into infrastructure, residential housing, and equipment. The local governments are even more zealous in capital spending because large projects are symbols of their performance; they get credits for big building projects in their local areas, but they are not actually held accountable for the costs of these projects. The funds for the investment often come from the loans by the local state-owned banks. If the loans finally go bad, it is hard to pin down who was responsible for the bad decision, and the state eventually picks up the tab. The true scales of construction and other investment projects are even larger than the reported figures in the official statistics, as the local officials always underreport their investment to avoid the discipline from the central government's macroeconomic contractionary measures.

The money for capital investment comes from public and private savings in China, which accounts for more than half (52 percent) of the GDP. For each yuan the Chinese made, they spent less than half in consumption. Why is the savings rate so high in China? Scholars give a list of explanations in line with conventional theories, which include the following:

- Rapid growth in income. As personal income rises rapidly, old habits remain, hence consumption increase lags behind income increase.

- A relatively younger population composition, so the larger working population provides a "demographic dividend."

- The influence of the Confucian culture and thrifty habits by the older generations.

- Lack of social security and high medical costs and costs of education for children, so households have to engage in a lot of precautionary saving.

Politicians and news media in the United States often blame undervalued Chinese currency for the huge U.S. trade deficit with China, though the majority of economists would consider a lower gross savings rate as a more important factor for the U.S. trade deficit. Is the Chinese RMB undervalued? Chang, based on his own research, estimates that the Chinese currency is 25 percent undervalued against the U.S. dollar, but 17 percent undervalued against the global balance equilibrium value, because the U.S. dollar is about 10 percent overvalued against its global balance equilibrium value. China's trade surplus with the United States is particularly large because, unlike the Euro zone and Japan, China keeps the RMB relatively stable with the U.S. dollar, thus reducing the foreign exchange cost in trade between China and the United States. Another reason is that China's export involves mostly processing, which employs goods and services produced in other countries, as is detailed in Koopman's chapter.

While China has the potential to be a great power, it faces serious challenges in both the economic and political arenas. With a population of 1.3 billion people, China is still poor in terms of per capita income. In other vital measures, in per capita terms, China appears weak, too. For example, China's per capita renewable water resources are only 20 percent of those of the United States, and per capita energy consumption is about 15 percent. To curb the population growth, China's fertility rate dropped to 1.54 in 2010. The population will age quickly in the coming years. This sets up a "demographic time bomb" for the future.

By the year 2050, the elderly would make up more than 30 percent of the population, and the dependency ratio would reach 80 percent.

To sustain its growth, China clearly has to move away from the current labor-intensive mode of development to a more technology-intensive economy, and it needs to increase highly skilled human capital. Yet, the current state-controlled education and science and technology systems do not promote creative thinking and research and development, which are crucial for sustained growth. Under the current system, science and technology rewards and research grants are often allocated based on who has political influences or personal connections rather than on merit. Intellectual property rights are not effectively protected, discouraging costly but valuable inventions and original innovations. China's technology right now is far behind the United States. With such an inefficient and even corrupted system, the gaps in advanced areas are not likely to close in the near future.

China's income gap is widening, frequently causing social and political conflict and unrest. The Gini index, a common indicator of inequality (to be explained in Chapter 4 by Terry Sicular), reaches 0.469 for China, which is higher than most countries in the world. The Chinese Communist government lacks the legitimacy to rule because it is not elected by people, and the people have little confidence in it. There is no independent legal system or channel where people can vent their grievances or trust that they will be treated fairly. Hence, there exists widespread hostility and distrust among people toward the governments and their officials, resulting in many protests and plenty of unrest. China is politically unstable under the current system, and a large-scale protest that topples the government is not entirely impossible in the future.

The Communist political authoritarian system is an inherently and intrinsically unstable system under which China lacks rule of law. The party determines everything, hence impeding not only creativity and independent thinking, but also entrepreneurship. Even worse, private property is still not genuinely protected. If the Communist authoritarian system were to collapse, the resulting political upheaval and economic crisis could dwarf any scale of economic recession.

As Chang points out, the income gap between the rich and the poor has been widening and has become an important factor for social instability. Terry Sicular's chapter, "Winners and Losers in China's Economic Reform," addresses this issue in greater detail, especially recent trends in inequality in China.

China has undoubtedly become more prosperous during the past three decades. However, dramatic policy and structure shifts, while bringing about tremendous benefits and wealth, inevitably create winners and losers. Economists have long thought that economic development is initially accompanied by rising inequality, but that eventually various forces emerge that will cause inequality to decline. This "inverted U" relationship between growth and inequality was first proposed by Simon Kuznets (1955) and is called the Kuznets hypothesis. The reasoning is that initially growth begins in certain sectors and regions, and the benefits of early growth therefore go to a small subset of the population, causing inequality to increase. As development continues, however, under the right conditions growth will spread to other sectors and regions. Employment will expand, and the benefits of growth will be shared more widely. In the long term, inequality can decline. Rising inequality is therefore not necessarily a permanent feature of growth in general, or growth in China.

A commonly used measure of inequality, as explained in Sicular's chapter, is the Gini coefficient, an index that takes a value of between 0 and 1. A Gini of 0 would mean perfect equality—all members of the society have identical, equal income. A Gini of 1 would indicate perfect inequality—one person has all of the society's income, and everyone else has zero income. The Gini coefficients for actual countries mostly range from 0.20 to 0.70.

Between 1995 and 2002 inequality in China remained roughly constant. Rural off-farm employment became more widespread, contributing to a decline in rural inequality. Macroeconomic growth during this period was widely shared. Nevertheless, other disequalizing factors—the urban-rural gap and education-based income disparities—continued. From 2002 to 2007 inequality resumed its upward trend. It appears that China had not yet reached the Kuznets turning point. By 2007, in fact, inequality in China had reached a level that was quite high by international standards; China's Gini coefficient was 0.497, which was near that of Mexico and Zambia, two countries that are considered to be high inequality.

Several factors appear to have contributed to the upward trend in inequality between 2002 and 2007. The gap between urban and rural incomes continued to widen, although within rural and urban areas, levels of inequality did not increase substantially. In 2007 urban incomes per capita on average were 4.1 times rural incomes. This ratio was up from 3.3 in 2002, which was already high by international standards.

A second factor contributing to increasing inequality has been the household income derived from assets and property. In the 1990s major property rights reforms were implemented that gave households opportunities to own property. These reforms included the privatization of urban housing, the development of the urban real estate market, enterprise ownership reforms, and the expansion of stock and financial markets. In the wake of these and other measures, household income from assets and property, including imputed rents from owner-occupied housing, rose to 10 percent of household income in 2002 and to 15 percent in 2007. Asset income in China is unequally distributed, and its contribution to inequality has increased. A decomposition of income by source reveals that the contribution of income from assets and property to national inequality increased considerably from 9 percent in 2002 to 20 percent in 2007.

The rise in inequality between 2002 and 2007 implies that some households benefited more and others less from growth during this period. Who, then, were the winners and losers? Sicular examines the growth in household income by decile groups in the population. All decile groups, from the poorest 10 percent of the population at the far left to the richest 10 percent at the far right, enjoyed positive growth in income between the two years. Growth in income of the poorest decile, however, was much smaller (in both percentage and absolute terms) than that of the richest decile. Income of the poorest decile increased by 406 yuan, less than 50 percent of 2002 income. Income of the richest decile roughly doubled, with an increase of nearly 16,000 yuan. For intermediate deciles, growth in income was correlated closely to their position in the income distribution.

Both the number of poor and the poverty rate declined dramatically between the early 1990s and early 2000s. In 1993 the poverty rate was 40 percent, but by 2002 it had fallen to 15 percent. The poverty rate declined further between 2002 and 2007 to about 4 percent. Most of this decline is due to a steep reduction in rural poverty. China's success in reducing poverty is outstanding by international standards. As a consequence of these trends, China has changed from a high-poverty country to a moderately low-poverty country. Moreover, China's share of world poverty has declined substantially, from nearly 40 percent of the world's poor in 1990 to only 15 percent in 2005. In conclusion, China's economic reforms have had many "winners" and few absolute "losers." Yet, challenges to China's harmonious society remain acute and ongoing.

The rapid growth of the Chinese economy has been fueled by a large-scale migration from the countryside to the cities. As China relies on cheap labor and labor-intensive manufacturing as key factors for development, tens of millions of migrant workers pour into coastal developmental areas looking for factory jobs, which pay wages higher than they can earn in the countryside. The most recent census (2010) estimates that there are now nearly 200 million rural migrants in urban China. The sheer scale of the migration has brought about profound changes in the economic, social, and demographic structures of the nation. Migrant workers bring back to their rural hometown not only earned wealth, but also experiences and expectations they gain while living in the urban areas. These experiences will change their frame of reference, especially that of their children. They will no longer be content with earning higher income—they want the same comfortable and rich life that the urban residents do. Mary Gallagher, in her chapter titled "Changes in the World's Workshop: The Demographic, Social, and Political Factors behind China's Labor Movement," offers insights on changes of the frame of reference of migrant workers, especially the younger generation, and the social and political impacts.

Gallagher explains that China's labor markets are highly segmented by institutional barriers to labor mobility across regions and across sectors. The *hukou* system, a restrictive residency registration system, is still fundamental in placing barriers between the labor markets of urban and rural citizens. There are also important social and cultural expectations about employment that further segment labor markets. Unemployed college graduates and unemployed rural migrants rarely compete in the same labor markets. There are some jobs that urban youth simply do not consider. Conversely, few employers in labor-intensive manufacturing would want to hire urban youth, who might not work hard enough or be able to withstand the harsh conditions. Barriers to labor mobility and segmentation based on *hukou* status and education level continue to exist in China, to the extent that sometimes labor shortages and labor surplus can coexist. For example, there were reports in the Chinese media in 2003 of a "migrant labor shortage" in development zones in China's south. Although this shortage ebbed during the global financial crisis and China's export crisis of 2008–2009, these shortages began to reappear soon after.

Migration, together with the one-child policy, has had transformative effects on the social and cultural characteristics of China's new generation of migrants. Gallagher finds that migrant workers born in the 1980s and after are markedly different in basic characteristics, in political socialization, and in life experiences from that of their parents. This generation is the first to be affected by the strict one-child policy that was implemented in the late 1970s. While in their parents' generation a family might have several children, even rural children in this generation generally share at most one sibling. In urban areas, the majority of children born are the only child in the family. Given their greater importance to the family's economy and long-term success, these "little emperors" have been lavished with attention and opportunity. Even rural children, who do not have the same educational and economic opportunities of their urban counterparts, have been given more attention and more protection from hard agricultural labor than in previous generations. Many rural parents understand that education is still the key to upward social mobility for their children. This focus on education has spared children from backbreaking manual labor and allowed them to focus on their studies. Although rural children do not attain the same level of education as urban children, they now have much higher rates of middle school and high school completion. Even if they take manufacturing jobs in the urban areas, they take it as part of their "going out" strategy for the transition to urban life.

The post–1980s generation, both rural and urban, is also markedly different from the previous generation in terms of political socialization and life experiences under socialism. As children of the reform era, they have little familiarity with the mass political campaigns of the high Mao Era. Their primary years of education and political socialization coincided with post–Tiananmen China, when economic growth was the major goal. The private sector was allowed to expand, and the "rule by law" campaign was disseminated in the media, encouraging people to protect their legal rights.

These different demographic characteristics and life experiences have helped create a new generation of migrants who are challenging traditional barriers and identities that have existed in China since the Maoist *hukou* policy was put into place in the late 1950s. Three main characteristics of this new generation are worth examining here: 1) their frame of reference, 2) their long-term expectations, and 3) their potential capacity to organize their interests and grievances collectively.

Surveys and interviews show that young rural migrants are increasingly better integrated and familiar with global youth culture and Chinese urban culture. Their frame of reference is increasingly not what would have happened to them if they had stayed in the countryside but what is possible for them as young urban citizens. This change in their reference point translates into higher expectations on the job and some tendency to value work that offers future opportunity even at the expense of current lower pays.

Given the higher levels of education in the current generation, better access to technology, and increased integration into urban culture, there is greater potential for this generation to articulate collective interests and to act collectively to promote and press for their interests and rights, vis-à-vis employers and the government alike. In the strikes of 2010, analysts pointed to workers' new abilities to organize within single workplaces and to design institutions to allow for leadership selection and representation. The increased potential for young migrants' collective power has been recognized in the media and by the governments. Since 2003, the party-state has been much more concerned about the conditions and long-term development of China's urbanizing citizens.

Migrant workers, mostly young adults, earn higher incomes than when they were in the countryside and substantially improve their lives, but what happens to those who stay behind in the rural areas, mostly older peasants? Would the movement of young rural adults to urban and coastal areas for higher-income-earning opportunities leave the older residents remaining in rural areas at greater risk of falling into poverty? John Giles addresses this issue in his chapter, "Left Behind in Old Age? Sources of Support for China's Rural Elderly in a Period of Growth, Migration, and Demographic Transition."

In general, rural residents lack access to pension support when they are of retirement age, and they must rely on either their own labor income or support from family members. In rural China, financial support for the elderly remains the responsibility of adult children and is even codified into laws governing the family. As the population of potential care providers continues to shrink as a result of both China's demographic transition and the availability of attractive migrant employment opportunities for the young, many observers have expressed concerns for the well-being of the rural elderly.

Giles points out that major differences exist in the primary sources of support for China's urban and rural elderly, and between men and women from both groups of elderly. While pensions are the single most significant source of support for the urban elderly, they remain a very minor source of support for the rural elderly. Labor income is the primary source of support for 37.9 percent of the rural elderly. Support through antipoverty programs does not figure prominently, because the rural *dibao* (benefits for low-income residents) was not an important source of income support for rural elderly households. Also notable is the inability of the elderly to earn income from property. The elderly in China have not grown old in an environment in which they could accumulate land wealth. Lack of land wealth limits the ability of the elderly to earn income from rents and may also limit the scope for encouraging intergenerational transfers from their children (who would be prospective heirs).

Giles further examines the sources of support by gender among the rural elderly. Family support is more important for rural elderly women, and labor income remains more important for men. His research finds that 68.5 percent of rural women over 60 report that financial support from family members is their most important source of support, whereas only 27.5 percent report that labor income is most important. By contrast, 48.5 percent of rural elderly men report that labor income remains their most important source of support, and only 39.3 percent report support from family members. When distinguishing the importance of pension by gender, a significantly higher share of rural men (8.1 percent) than women (1.3 percent) report that pension income is their most significant source of financial support. The gap between men and women reflects historical differences between genders in employment in local government and the military.

Given the structure of elderly support, Giles finds that the effects of lost farm income and uncertainty about land tenure likely dominate the effects of increased income from remittances in labor supply decisions of the rural elderly. Nonetheless, this effect is not statistically significant for men or for women under 70. Women over 70, however, are 8 percent more likely to continue working (most likely in agriculture) if the household has a migrant child. The elderly have to work more to make up the income loss. Women over 70 with a migrant child work 411 hours more during a year, or the equivalent of 10 40-hour workweeks. For regions of the country planting two crops a year, this would amount to full-time work during the agricultural busy season.

Overall, migrant children continue to provide remittance support to their parents. On average, the predicted transfer from adult children is sufficient to maintain elderly incomes above the poverty line. However, as the range of potential transfers is wide, elderly people with migrant children face greater risk of falling below the poverty line. Migration of adult children may also have a significant impact on the work status of elderly women. Having a migrant child in the family raises the probability that a woman over 70 will still be in the labor force and work longer hours. For men and women under 70, a migrant child has a positive but statistically insignificant effect on participation in income-earning activities.

What is the long-term outlook of the Chinese economy? Can China maintain the momentum and sustain this phenomenal growth well into the next several decades? A team of elite World Bank economists projects that China's yearly growth rate will "slow down" to 5.9 percent in 2021 and further down to 5 percent in 2026 (World Bank 2012). This projection is remarkably close to Dr. Zhiwu Chen's one-man projection when he delivered the lecture "China in 2049" in 2011 at Western Michigan University. The final chapter of this volume is a short transcribed version of his lecture.

Chen presents a "big picture" of a possible future GDP path for China in comparison to the United States from 2011 to 2049, the centennial of the founding of People's Republic of China. He depicts three phases of China's growth path: an annual growth rate of 8.5 percent from 2011 to 2016 in the first phase, a drop in growth by 12 percent in 2017 in the second phase (a bold projection with reasons given in the chapter, unlike projections by other agencies such as IMF), followed by a resumption of a steady growth rate of 5–6 percent per year through 2049 in the third phase. Chen predicts that in 2049, when PRC is 100 years old, China's nominal GDP will surpass the United States, and if purchasing power parity is taken into account, China's GDP will surpass the United States much earlier, in 2027, 15 years from now.

Chen gives a very long-run historical perspective of China's per capita GDP over 2000 years and notes that the high growth actually only occurred in the last 40 years. He gives an insightful analysis of China's rapid growth and ascent in the recent decades. He refutes the conventional wisdom that the main driving factor of China's rise is an abundant and low-cost workforce (reasons given in the chapter). He convincingly argues that China has ascended by "riding the tide," benefiting from the world's encouraging trade environment because of increasing globalization and dispersion of technological progress as a result of industrial revolution. Chen concludes by pointing out some challenges and concerns for China's sustainable growth, such as over-reliance of growth on state capitalism, that is, government dominance in the past and current growth of the economy.

The chapters in this volume reflect the opinions of six leading experts on certain important aspects and issues of the Chinese economy and its economic relations with the United States. While these chapters can cover only part of the complex pictures, they all contain insightful analyses of the issues concerned. The analytical frameworks and the insights presented in this volume will be valuable for understanding and evaluating the Chinese economy, its growth, and its relations with the United States, which hopefully will help guide policymakers in this ever-integrated global economy.

References

Kuznets, Simon. 1955. "Economic Growth and Income Inequality." *American Economic Review* 65(1): 1–28.

World Bank. 2012. *China 2030: Building a Modern, Harmonious and Creative High-Income Society*. Washington, DC: World Bank.

2

U.S.-China Economic Relations and Value Chains in Global Production Networks

Robert B. Koopman
U.S. International Trade Commission

During the past 15 years trade between the United States and China has grown substantially. This trade growth has increased the economic interdependence between the two countries, resulting in benefits for both, while also creating some economic tensions. China has experienced rapid economic growth and development with substantial decreases in poverty and increases in per capita GDP, which many academics attribute to China's market-driven economic reforms and its related integration with the world economy. Up until the 2008 financial crisis, the U.S. economy experienced a long period of relatively strong growth through increased productivity and improved integration of information and computer technologies, as well as strong consumption growth accompanied by a declining national savings rate. While U.S. consumption-led growth benefited from inexpensive goods from China such as consumer electronics and textiles, it has also resulted in growing bilateral imbalances.

U.S. import growth from China has slowed over the last several years because of weak U.S. economic growth, a drop in the value of the dollar, and a decline in imbalances. This chapter focuses on the period prior to the financial crisis, as it aligns well with recent research on value-added trade, which is discussed in a later section.

Researchers and policymakers have focused on three broad areas to explain the increasing trade imbalance between the two countries and, more recently, China's growing trade surplus with the world. The first area is China's extensive use of policy instruments to encourage its rapid economic development and transition from a centrally planned economy to a market-driven economy.[1] These policies include, among others, incentives for foreign investment and export performance, the establishment of special economic zones and substantial infrastructure investment, and a fixed exchange rate. A second explanation focuses on more macroeconomic factors, suggesting that significant imbalance in the U.S. savings and investment rates, combined with relatively rapid consumption-led economic growth in the United States compared to other developed countries, have led to an increased current account and merchandise trade imbalance.[2] A third area has been the rapid growth in fragmented global production processes, as businesses take advantage of declining information and communications technology costs, and international logistics costs to distribute pieces of their production chain based on lowest cost sources (Dean, Fung, and Wang 2011; Hummels, Ishii, and Yi 2001; Yi 2003). Although fragmentation of global production has developed independently of China's policy environment and is a widespread phenomenon, a large part of China's growth in exports to the United States has been in processing trade carried out by foreign-invested enterprises (FIEs), many of which have benefited from China's pro FIE and pro "imports for exports" policies.[3]

In this chapter I present a summary of the U.S.-China trade relationship prior to 2008 and describe some of the driving factors underlying the rapid growth in U.S.-China trade. I then present data on the World Trade Organization (WTO) and U.S. import injury cases that support the notion that, from the U.S. perspective, trade relations with China are treated much like those with our long-term historical economic and political partners such as the European Union (EU) and North American Free Trade Agreement (NAFTA) countries. Finally, I discuss current research on value-added trade that could be important from a future policy perspective in understanding global value chains and China's position in them.

AN OVERVIEW OF THE U.S.-CHINA TRADE RELATIONSHIP

Figures 2.1 and 2.2 summarize U.S. merchandise trade shifts with the world and with China between 2002 and 2006. The overall U.S. merchandise trade deficit increased to $915.6 billion in 2006. The long-term trend in the U.S. trade deficit remains a key policy concern for the

Figure 2.1 Overall Shifts in U.S. Merchandise Trade through 2006

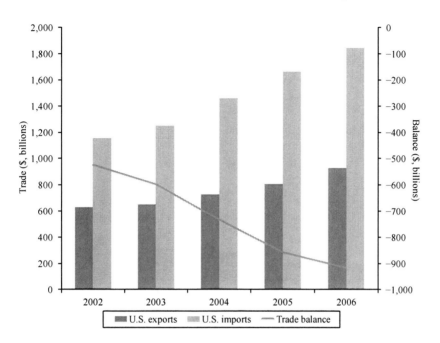

SOURCE: USITC.

United States and its global trading and financial partners. China's rapidly increasing share in the merchandise trade deficit—it reached $235 billion in 2006—has raised particular concern. The factors and trends driving U.S. merchandise trade were numerous. Economic growth in the United States and its major trading partners contributed to increased bilateral merchandise trade flows in 2006, while strong growth in consumer spending, business structures investment, and exports supported the economic performance of the United States.[4] The rate of increase in the U.S. merchandise trade deficit slowed from 17 percent in 2005 to 7 percent in 2006, even as the deficit grew from $858.4 billion in 2005 to a record $915.6 billion in 2006. Total U.S. exports increased to a record $929.5 billion, a 16 percent increase. Aircraft, spacecraft, and related equipment; motor vehicles; and petroleum products recorded the largest sector increases for a combined $33.5 billion (27 percent)

Figure 2.2 Shifts in U.S.-China Merchandise Trade through 2006

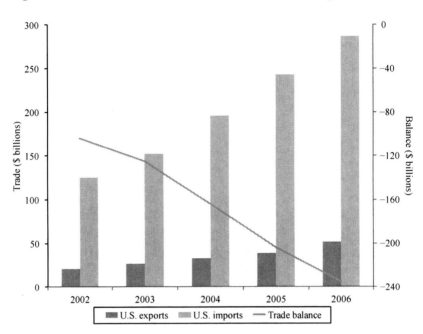

SOURCE: USITC.

of export growth, although export increases are recorded in every merchandise sector. Meanwhile, U.S. imports for all merchandise sectors increased by 11 percent to a record $1.8 trillion. The energy products, minerals and metals, and transportation equipment sectors accounted for over half of the increase. The crude petroleum, motor vehicles, and petroleum products commodity groups recorded the largest increases in 2006, accounting for a third of import growth.

The U.S.-China trade relationship continues to evolve quickly. The U.S. merchandise trade deficit with China rose for the fifth straight year, increasing by 16 percent to $235.4 billion, reflecting the continued U.S. demand for goods produced in China. China is the fourth-largest export market for the United States and the second-leading import source in terms of absolute value. The continued rapid economic growth in China, coupled with China's increasing role as a low-cost production location, contributed to the expansion in U.S.-China trade in 2006. U.S. exports to China rose at a greater rate than the preceding years, by $12.8 billion, or 33 percent. The most significant increases in U.S. exports were in electronic products ($3.2 billion), transportation equipment ($2.5 billion), and minerals and metals ($2.5 billion). Increased demand for computer and telecommunications products by U.S. consumers contributed to continued growth in U.S. imports from China, increasing by $6.3 billion (16 percent) and $3.7 billion (26 percent), respectively. In 2006, the U.S. telecommunications market grew at the fastest rate since 2000, with demand for services such as broadband leading to increased demand for telecommunications and network equipment.

Changes in the Composition of U.S. Trade

While much attention has been paid to the increasing merchandise trade imbalance with China, it is useful to consider this trade relationship in a broader context. Table 2.1 shows the changes in the composition of U.S. non-oil imports with a number of its main trading partners between 1989 and 2007. China's share of U.S. imports increased from 2.8 percent to 20.6 percent, displacing Japan as the United States' second-largest import source after NAFTA. During this period China became the largest single import source country for the United States.

In 1989, imports from the United States' largest Asian partners (Japan, China, Korea, Taiwan, Malaysia, and Singapore) accounted for 43.9 percent of U.S. non-oil imports. By 2007, the same share had dropped slightly, to 41.5 percent of U.S. non-oil imports. During this period, the U.S. share of imports from many of its other Asian partners declined. Between 1989 and 2007, the combined share of Japan, Korea, Taiwan, Malaysia, Singapore, and other Asian countries in U.S. non-oil imports dropped from 41.1 percent to 20.9 percent. Thus, much of China's increasing share of U.S. non-oil imports came at the expense of other Asian countries, particularly Japan, which dropped from 22 percent to 8.9 percent of U.S. non-oil imports during the same period.

While the total value of non-oil imports from Asia grew substantially, its share of total non-oil imports remained fairly constant, reflecting substantial growth of imports from other regions as well. This phenomenon is particularly interesting because the composition of U.S. imports from Asia changed substantially, as more and more of the share of U.S. non-oil imports from Asia came from China.

Table 2.1 U.S. Import Shares by Country, 1989–2007

Year	Rest of world	NAFTA	Rest of Asia	Japan	China	EU15
1989	10.9	24.0	19.1	22.0	2.8	21.1
1990	11.0	24.3	18.5	20.8	3.5	21.9
1991	11.0	24.4	18.6	21.1	4.4	20.6
1992	11.3	24.5	18.4	20.1	5.5	20.2
1993	11.4	25.2	17.8	20.2	6.2	19.2
1994	11.7	26.2	17.5	19.3	6.5	18.7
1995	11.7	27.0	17.9	17.8	6.8	18.7
1996	11.9	28.3	17.4	15.9	7.3	19.2
1997	12.4	28.4	16.8	15.1	8.0	19.3
1998	12.6	28.7	16.0	14.1	8.5	20.2
1999	12.2	29.4	15.8	13.7	8.9	20.0
2000	12.6	29.1	16.1	13.4	9.5	19.3
2001	12.7	29.3	14.7	12.3	10.3	20.7
2002	12.8	28.5	14.5	11.5	12.3	20.5
2003	13.3	27.0	14.0	10.6	14.2	20.8
2004	13.7	26.5	13.7	10.1	15.9	20.1
2005	13.9	25.8	12.9	9.8	17.9	19.8
2006	14.1	25.3	12.7	9.6	19.2	19.2
2007	13.7	25.1	12.0	8.9	20.6	19.6

NOTE: U.S. imports, except Chapter 27, in percentage of total.
SOURCE: USITC and author's calculations.

A similar pattern arose in U.S. non-oil export shares (see Table 2.2). The NAFTA partner countries held a fairly constant share of U.S. non-oil exports between 1989 and 2007, while large Asian countries' shares declined from 29.2 percent to 25.7 percent of U.S. non-oil exports. As with imports, a fairly substantial shift occurred between exports to Japan and China. In 1989, Japan accounted for 12.1 percent of U.S. non-oil exports and China 1.7 percent. By 2007, Japan had dropped to 5.7 percent and China climbed to 6.0 percent.

Driving Factors in U.S.-China Bilateral Trade

In general, bilateral trade between the United States and China was driven by FIEs, and more recently from a growing role by private firms operating in China (see Figure 2.3). Electronic machinery (HS-84) con-

Table 2.2 U.S. Export Shares by Country, 1989–2007

Year	Rest of world	NAFTA	Rest of Asia	Japan	China	EU15
1989	17.4	28.5	15.4	12.1	1.7	24.9
1990	16.7	28.3	15.2	12.3	1.3	26.1
1991	17.9	28.0	15.6	11.5	1.6	25.4
1992	18.9	29.1	15.6	10.8	1.7	23.9
1993	19.4	30.2	16.2	10.5	2.0	21.7
1994	17.7	31.8	16.9	10.6	1.9	21.0
1995	18.0	29.0	18.4	11.2	2.2	21.2
1996	18.7	29.9	17.9	11.0	2.1	20.5
1997	19.0	31.5	17.4	9.7	2.0	20.5
1998	18.9	33.5	14.7	8.7	2.2	22.2
1999	16.6	35.2	15.5	8.5	2.0	22.2
2000	15.6	35.6	16.4	8.6	2.2	21.6
2001	16.9	34.9	15.1	8.1	2.7	22.3
2002	16.0	36.0	15.7	7.7	3.3	21.2
2003	15.6	35.3	15.9	7.6	4.2	21.5
2004	16.5	34.9	15.9	7.0	4.6	21.1
2005	17.9	34.9	15.0	6.5	5.0	20.6
2006	19.3	33.4	14.7	6.1	5.7	20.7
2007	21.7	31.4	14.0	5.7	6.0	21.1

SOURCE: USITC.

stituted the largest and fastest growing product category for both imports and exports (see Tables 2.3A and B). In addition, China's government incentive schemes, such as Economic and Technological Development Zones and other specialized zones, played a dominant role in China's imports from the United States (see Figure 2.3 and Tables 2.3A and 2.3B).[5]

China's trade pattern with the United States differs in some respects from its trade pattern with the world. Yao (2008) finds that while China ran a large trade surplus with the United States in machinery and electrical products, it ran a substantial deficit with the rest of the world in these products, and that China's special economic zones played an important role in these trade flows. This, along with the general realignment of U.S. import shares from Asia discussed above, supports the argument that China is playing an important role as an assembly platform for Asia by importing electronic components and shipping final

Figure 2.3 Disaggregating China-U.S. Trade by Enterprise Type, Customs Regime, and Incentive Scheme

China's Exports to the U.S. by Incentive Scheme

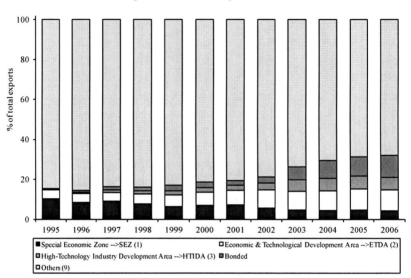

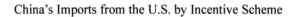

China's Imports from the U.S. by Incentive Scheme

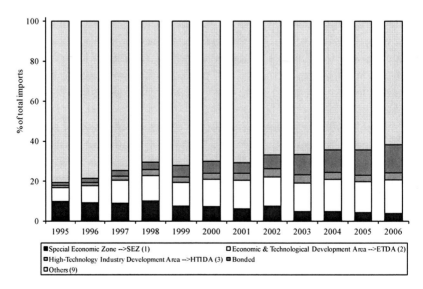

Figure 2.3 (continued)

China's Exports to the U.S. by Enterprise Type

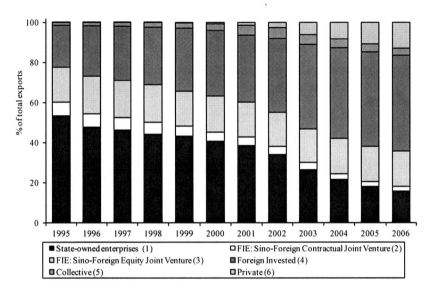

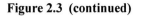

China's Imports from the U.S. by Enterprise Type

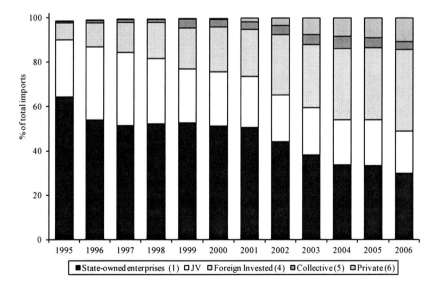

Figure 2.3 (continued)

China's Exports to the U.S. by Trade Mode

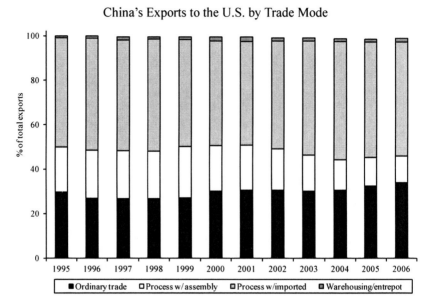

China's Imports from the U.S. by Trade Mode

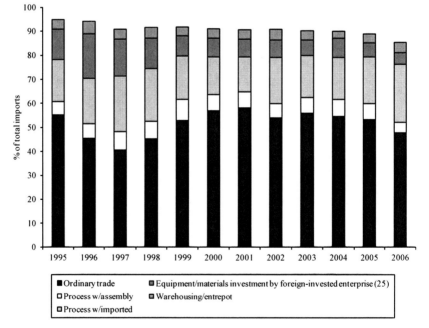

SOURCE: Ferrantino et al. (2010).

Table 2.3A Decomposing China's Top 20 Traded Products with the United States: U.S. Exports to China ($, millions)

Rank (2006)	HS[a]	Product	1995 Value	1995 % of total	2006 Value	2006 % of total
1	85	Electrical machinery and associated parts	1,270	11	10,178	18
2	84	Machinery and associated parts	2,190	19	7,704	14
3	88	Aircraft, spacecraft, and associated parts	1,176	10	6,090	11
4	90	Optical/photographic, medical, or surgical instruments and parts	450	4	2,941	5
5	39	Plastics and articles thereof	351	3	2,716	5
6	12	Oil seeds, grains, and fruits	56	0	2,585	5
7	52	Cotton, including yarns and woven fabrics	834	7	2,082	4
8	72	Iron and steel	141	1	1,800	3
9	74	Copper and associated articles	146	1	1,774	3
10	76	Aluminum and associated articles	147	1	1,735	3
11	47	Wood pulp; recovered (waste and scrap) paper and paperboard	184	2	1,474	3
12	29	Organic chemicals	263	2	1,418	3
13	87	Vehicles, nonrailway	172	1	1,291	2
14	41	Raw hides, skins, and leather	111	1	876	2
15	28	Inorganic chemicals; organic or inorganic compounds of precious metals	39	0	687	1
16	81	Base metals, cermets, and associated articles	10	0	677	1
17	38	Miscellaneous chemical products	105	1	669	1
18	44	Wood and articles of wood; wood charcoal	29	0	551	1
19	98	Special classification provisions, nesoi	148	1	483	1
20	48	Paper and paperboard; articles of paper pulp, paper or paperboard	142	1	466	1
		Subtotal	7,963	68	48,198	87
		Total	11,748		55,224	

**Table 2.3B Decomposing China's Top 20 Traded Products with the
United States: U.S. Imports from China ($, millions)**

Rank (2006)	HS[a]	Product	1995 Value	1995 % of total	2006 Value	2006 % of total
1	85	Electrical machinery and associated parts	7,886	17	64,906	23
2	84	Machinery and associated parts	3,624	8	62,266	22
3	95	Toys, games, and sports equipment	6,222	14	20,892	7
4	94	Furniture; bedding, cushions, and lamps	1,979	4	19,358	7
5	64	Footwear	5,824	13	13,890	5
6	62	Articles of apparel and clothing accessories	3,277	7	11,858	4
7	73	Articles of iron or steel	556	1	8,367	3
8	61	Articles of apparel and clothing accessories	1,376	3	8,010	3
9	39	Plastics and articles thereof	1,623	4	7,465	3
10	42	Articles of leather	2,536	6	6,835	2
11	87	Vehicles, nonrailway	501	1	5,134	2
12	90	Optical/photographic, medical, or surgical instruments and parts	1,274	3	4,787	2
13	63	Textile articles	645	1	4,628	2
14	44	Wood and articles of wood; wood charcoal	225	0	2,997	1
15	83	Miscellaneous articles of base metal	324	1	2,982	1
16	71	Natural or cultured pearls, stones, precious metals	248	1	2,564	1
17	99	Special import reporting provisions, nesoi	202	0	2,502	1
18	40	Rubber and articles thereof	138	0	2,472	1
19	29	Organic chemicals	360	1	2,258	1
20	72	Iron and steel	198	0	2,176	1
		Subtotal	39,018	86	256,348	89
		Total	45,555		287,773	

[a] HS = Harmonized system code.
SOURCE: USITC Dataweb. This is an update from a table in Hammer (2006).

assembled goods to the United States. Hummels, Ishii, and Yi (2001) and Dean, Fung, and Wang (2011) show that a significant share of China's export values reflect content imported from other countries and reexported after some transformation.

There has been a broad debate on the driving factors behind the rapidly growing U.S.-China trade relationship (Ahearne et al. 2007; Fosler and Bottelier 2007; Branstetter and Lardy 2006; Dean, Fung, and Wang 2011; Hummels, Ishii, and Yi 2001; and Yi 2003). An extensive discussion of that debate is beyond the scope of this chapter. Instead I will discuss how this rapidly growing economic relationship generated trade tensions between the two countries, as represented by the United States' use of international WTO dispute settlement panels and national antidumping (AD) cases, and then present a summary of a novel method for looking more closely at this trade relationship that better reflects global supply chains.

The United States, China, and the WTO

As part of an internal U.S. political economy debate and compromise, Congress and the president agreed to changes in U.S. import safeguard mechanisms such as AD and import surge protections, as the United States committed to reduced tariffs in the Kennedy Round of General Agreement on Tariffs and Trade (GATT) negotiations in 1967. As a result of that round and later GATT and WTO rounds, bilateral free trade agreements, and nonreciprocal tariff preference agreements, the U.S. average trade weighted tariff rate dropped significantly from roughly 12 percent to 5 percent between 1967 and the mid 1970s, and continued to drop to 1.3 percent for 2007 (Irwin [2005] and author's calculations). With the creation of the WTO in 1995, the United States has also made use of, and been the recipient of, formal dispute panels to resolve disagreements with its trading partners. These mechanisms are viewed as integral components of normal U.S. trade relations. In the next section I summarize data regarding the United States' use of WTO dispute panels and national AD cases during this period to illustrate the fact that trade disputes between the United States and China are not much different from those between the United States and its other large trading partners.

It is important to note some important differences between WTO dispute panels and the AD mechanism discussed below. World Trade Organization dispute cases are brought by one or more governments against another government, and the cases are heard in Geneva, Switzerland, by WTO dispute panels with three members chosen by the WTO. Antidumping cases in the United States are brought by one or more U.S. firms, or other nongovernmental interested parties, against one or more foreign firms. The cases are argued by private parties in Washington, DC, before two U.S. government agencies—the Department of Commerce to determine whether dumping is occurring, and the U.S. International Trade Commission to determine whether that dumping injures the U.S. firms. Thus it is inaccurate in the AD context to refer to U.S. cases against China, as the cases are brought by private parties before U.S. government panels.

U.S.-China Trade Tensions

The growing bilateral trade deficit between the United States and China has generated concern among policymakers in both countries. Numerous sources in China have expressed concern that the U.S. government is making extensive use of WTO dispute panels, that U.S. firms are making extensive use of AD injury cases, and that the use of these mechanisms has a negative impact on the two countries' "harmonious trade relations" (see, for example, China State Council [2005] and *China Daily* [2007a,b]). Many U.S. lawmakers and interest groups have called for the government to make more extensive use of WTO dispute panels and to make import injury mechanisms, such as AD, easier for U.S. firms to file, or to prove, and thus help slow the bilateral deficits' growth.[6]

Below I briefly review the use of these mechanisms in the United States vis-á-vis China and its firms and put them in a broader context for U.S. trade relations. Through 2008 the U.S. government's use of WTO cases and private firms' use of import injury cases (and the U.S. government's determinations in those cases) appear to not single out China or its firms. Instead, the broad data appear to show that China and its domestic firms were treated similarly to the United States and its other major trading partners and general political allies, such as its NAFTA partners and the EU.

WTO Dispute Settlement Cases

Between 1995, when the WTO was created, and 2008, the United States was a complainant in 86 dispute settlement consultations (see Table 2.4). The top five respondent countries are the European Economic Community, Mexico, Korea, Japan, and Canada—countries long considered U.S. political and economic partners. China ranks sixth, followed by India, Brazil, and Argentina. The pattern that emerges from this data is that the United States views WTO consultations as part of its normal trade relationship with its major political and economic partners, and that China and other developing countries with significant U.S. trade relations are treated similarly. This suggests that from a U.S. perspective, utilizing the WTO dispute settlement mechanism is a natural part of a robust economic relationship.

Since China joined the WTO in 2001, it has ranked second to the EU in terms of number of panels with the United States as a complainant, followed by Canada and Mexico (see Table 2.5). This probably reflects a combination of China's rapid growth to become a major trading partner for the United States. Recall that China's share of U.S. imports has risen dramatically, roughly doubling since its accession to the WTO, and surpassing the EU as the United States' second-largest trading partner. If we compare the rankings in Table 2.5 with the import shares in Table 2.1, the data suggest that from a U.S. perspective our trading tensions with China appear normal and on par with our main economic and political allies. While China has expressed that it desires harmonious trade relations with its partners, including the United States, from the U.S. perspective it would appear that through 2008, at the WTO, the United States has treated China as it would any other large trading partner.

Import Injury (AD) Cases

Firms in China remain a major target for AD cases around the world. According to the Global Trade Protection Report, 2,007 firms in China were the main target of AD cases between 1995 and 2006, with 540 investigations. Interestingly, U.S. firms ranked fourth being targeted in 172 cases, behind the EU and member states at 502 cases and South Korean firms with 228 cases.

Table 2.4 WTO Dispute Settlement Consultations, since WTO Established with the United States as Complainant, through 2008

Rank	Respondents	Total number of cases	% of total cases
1	EEC	16	18.4
2	Mexico	6	6.9
3	Korea	6	6.9
4	Japan	6	6.9
5	Canada	6	6.9
6	China	5	5.7
7	India	4	4.6
8	Brazil	4	4.6
9	Argentina	4	4.6
10	Philippines	3	3.4
11	Ireland	3	3.4
12	Belgium	3	3.4
13	Australia	3	3.4
14	Turkey	2	2.3
15	Greece	2	2.3
16	France	2	2.3
17	Venezuela	1	1.1
18	United Kingdom	1	1.1
19	Sweden	1	1.1
20	Romania	1	1.1
21	Portugal	1	1.1
22	Pakistan	1	1.1
23	Netherlands	1	1.1
24	Indonesia	1	1.1
25	Egypt	1	1.1
26	Denmark	1	1.1
27	Chile	1	1.1
	Totals	86	98.9

SOURCE: WTO. Data generated by Ted Wilson, Office of Economics, USITC. Percentage does not equal 100 due to rounding.

Table 2.5 WTO Dispute Settlement Consultations, since China's Accession with the United States as a Complainant, through 2008

Rank		Number	Percent
1	EEC	6	30.0
2	China	5	25.0
3	Canada	2	10.0
4	Mexico	2	10.0
5	Egypt	1	5.0
6	India	1	5.0
7	Japan	1	5.0
8	Turkey	1	5.0
9	Venezuela	1	5.0
	Totals	20	100.0

SOURCE: WTO. Data generated by Ted Wilson, Office of Economics, USITC.

I do not discuss or estimate the economic effects of AD actions, as that is beyond the scope of this chapter, but for a discussion of the potential economic impacts of AD actions see Blonigen and Prusa (2003). Examining U.S. AD data, we can see whether China's rapid trade growth with the United States led to a disproportionate number of AD investigations on firms in China, and/or a disproportionate amount of China's trade affected by AD findings. Table 2.6 shows that between 2001 and 2006, firms in China were respondents in 20 percent of all U.S. AD cases (more than any other country, but roughly in line with China's share of total U.S. non-oil imports), and that firms in China accounted for 31 percent of the affirmative determinations. Thus, while firms in China were named in new AD filings in proportion to China's U.S. import share, they were more likely than firms from other countries to be found causing injury to U.S. firms. For the longer 1980–2006 period, firms in China were a party in only 10.5 percent of the cases, so the share of cases involving China had definitely risen (see U.S. International Trade Commission [2008]).

The above discussion focuses on the injury determination of the AD process. The long-run average since 1980 is 37 percent of all AD/ countervailing duty (CVD) cases (42 percent for AD alone) being found in the affirmative, affecting 0.3 percent of total imports. Thus, China's recent experience is not out of line with the long-term findings for all countries. Also note that the dumping determination is handled by the

Table 2.6 Number of U.S. Antidumping Cases and Affirmative Findings, China and Total, 2001–2006

	Antidumping cases		Affirmative findings	
Year	China	Total	China	Total
2001	9	92	5	40
2002	8	35	6	12
2003	9	35	6	14
2004	9	34	8	20
2005	3	10	2	6
2006	4	8	2	2
Totals for period	42	214	29	94
Percent China		20		31

SOURCE: USITC data and author's calculations.

Department of Commerce, and its long-run average for affirmative findings of dumping is nearly 90 percent, while the ITC injury determination rate is much lower.

Another way to look at the treatment of firms from China in U.S. trade is the share of China's imports to the United States affected by AD cases. Irwin (2005) finds that rising U.S. AD activity on an aggregate level is related to the increase in import penetration, among other factors, and that the rise in import penetration is largely associated with falling U.S. import tariffs.

Figure 2.4 shows U.S. imports from the world plotted against those affected by new AD/CVD cases. Since 1980, there have been occasional spikes of around 1 percent of the value of imports affected by new AD/CVD duties; the long-run average, despite rapidly growing imports, is around 0.16 percent.

In Figure 2.5 we see that China's historical trade volume subjected to new U.S. AD duties tracked fairly closely with that of the world. Since 1980, there have been occasional spikes in activity of nearly 1 percent, thus similar to the world total, however the average over the period is 0.16 percent, which equals the world total for that period.

Figure 2.6 shows that, as with Irwin's findings, during the 1989–2007 period U.S. import tariffs for the world continued to decline, from 3.4 percent to 1.3 percent. Duties on imports from China fell from 8.5

Figure 2.4 U.S. Imports from the World, and Percentage Affected by Affirmative AD/CVD Findings

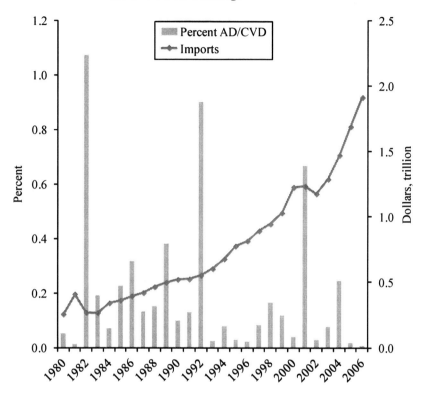

SOURCE: USITC data and author's calculations.

percent to 3.1 percent, representing the biggest decline among the countries and regions covered.[7] Such a decline in tariff rates and increased penetration is consistent with historical U.S. experience of rising AD activity.

U.S. imports from China have grown rapidly since its WTO accession, but in the aggregate firms in China appear to be treated in a quite similar respect to those in the rest of the world (see Figures 2.4 and 2.5). Between 2000 and 2006, less than 0.19 percent of total imports from China were subject to new affirmative determinations in the United States, while the world average was 0.14 percent. Both of these numbers represent a small fraction of U.S. imports. It is true that in

Figure 2.5 U.S. Imports from China, and Percentage Affected by Affirmative AD/CVD Findings

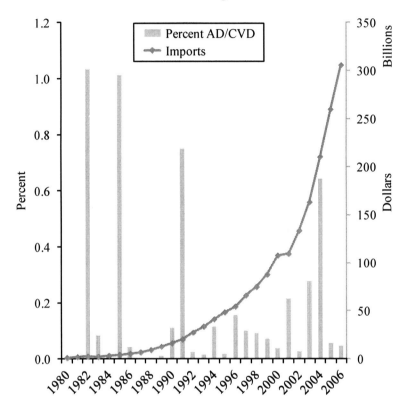

SOURCE: USITC and author's calculations.

the period 1980–1999, imports from China were much less affected by new AD cases in the United States than the world average. Imports from China during the pre-WTO accession era (1980–1990) averaged only 0.11 percent of import value subject to a new affirmative decision, while imports for the world over the same period averaged 0.18 percent. Thus, since WTO accession and 2006, China moved more in line with the average treatment in terms of U.S. imports subject to AD duties.

Thus, in terms of two measures of trade tensions, the numbers of WTO dispute settlement panels and the share of imports affected by import injury findings, we see that the United States largely treated

Figure 2.6 U.S. Average Duty Rates, by Country or Region, 1989–2007

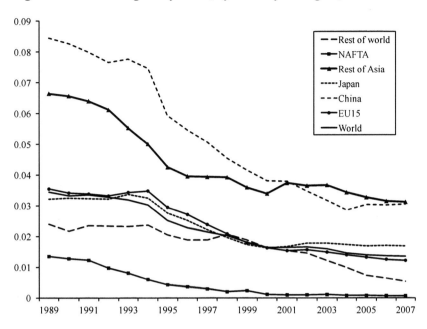

SOURCE: USITC and author's calculations.

China and its firms as it did any other major trading partner, including its main political and economic allies. In the United States, as in other countries, the number of AD cases brought against firms in China has been increasing, and the number of cases involving firms in China found affirmative in the injury phase has risen above the world average. These data suggest that China's concerns that U.S. actions in the WTO and in its national import injury cases indicate that the United States does not care about harmonious trade relations may be misplaced and simply reflect a difference in culture and expectations as to how each side defines harmonious and normal trade relations.

Apart from growing trade tensions, the rise of China as a supplier to the world is remarkable. The next part of this chapter focuses on a methodology to better understand how globalization—and the development of global value chains that appear to focus on China—may affect traditional gross trade values often used to describe bilateral trade relations. These insights, based on the domestic and foreign value embedded in gross trade data, suggest that the trade relationship between the United States and China is more complicated than traditional data suggest, and that Japan and other Asian countries export indirectly to the United States through China.

VALUE ADDED IN CHINESE EXPORTS

Recently, Pascal Lamy, director general of the WTO, suggested that ". . . by focusing on gross values of exports and imports, traditional trade statistics also give us a distorted picture of trade imbalances between countries." He argues that value-added trade statistics help reveal that the macroeconomic imbalances present in the current global economy are not likely to be corrected through focus on bilateral trade deficits (Lamy 2011).

In the United States there has been great political and press attention paid to the long-term current account deficit, and particularly the bilateral trade deficit with China. At the U.S. International Trade Commission, beginning shortly after China's accession to the WTO in the early 2000s, we started receiving requests from our governmental customers regarding the growing trade imbalance with China. We first gathered data similar to that seen in Figure 2.7, traditional import values showing rising imports from China, and much of the rest of the world in value terms. Of course, when the questions first came in we had not yet experienced the recession of 2008 related to the financial crisis, so the path of import growth was fairly steadily upward, except for the 2001 recession. We next transformed the data into shares as seen in Figure 2.8, which plainly shows that something important was going on in Asia, and that much of it was related to Asian supply chain realignment and a focus on China as a point of final assembly in those chains. However, we had no way of clearly showing these links in the aggregate data at that time. Groups highly critical of trade referred to data such as that in Figure 2.7 and generally focused on China for keeping its currency artificially low in order to increase exports to the United States, among other countries. Critics argued that since other Asian countries continued to expand exports to the United States, China's increased exports were essentially completely offsetting domestic production, not substi-

Figure 2.7 U.S. Imports from Asia, NAFTA, and the World, 1989–2009

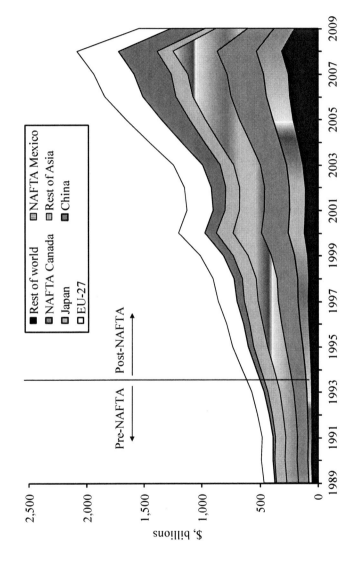

SOURCE: Author's calculations.

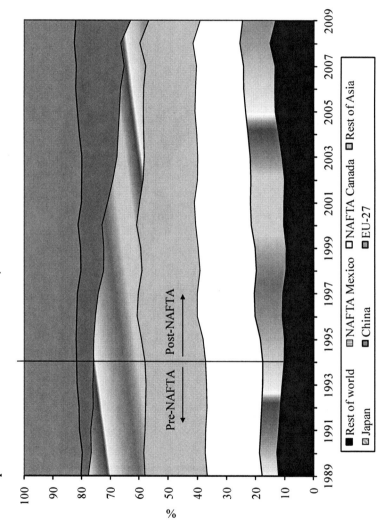

Figure 2.8 U.S. Imports Shares from Asia and NAFTA, 1989–2009

SOURCE: Author's calculations.

tuting for other Asian exports. Further, trade critics often pointed out that low prices from China, due to the currency undervaluation, stimulated demand in the United States for Chinese imports, and were then generating a growing current account deficit. To better address these kinds of comments we then developed data similar to that presented in Figure 2.9, which suggest that macro factors, particularly relatively strong economic growth—exhibited in this figure through a stable, low unemployment rate through most of the period, and relatively robust economic growth in the United States compared to other developed countries, combined with a low savings rate—were the main contributors to growing trade deficits. Despite the various forms of data presented, there was no clear "smoking gun" linking other Asian countries to Chinese exports. Similar arguments and concerns were expressed regarding NAFTA trade flows.

Methods for Understanding Domestic and Foreign Value Added in Trade

These efforts to inform our customers and the need to more fully understand what was happening in global trade flows led us to delve fairly deeply into value-added trade issues.[8] How would one assess foreign versus domestic content in a country's exports? In one of the literature's most influential papers, Hummels, Ishii, and Yi (2001; HIY in subsequent discussion) propose a method to decompose a country's exports into domestic and foreign value-added (FVA) share based on a country's input-output (IO) table. Hummels, Ishii, and Yi make a key assumption that the intensity in the use of imported inputs is the same between production for exports and production for domestic sales. However, this assumption is violated in the presence of processing exports, a prevalent part of China's export and import markets. Processing exports are characterized by imports for exports with favorable tariff treatment: firms import parts and other intermediate materials from abroad, with tariff exemptions on the imported inputs and other tax preferences from local or central governments, and, after processing or assembling, export the finished products. The policy preferences for processing exports usually lead to a significant difference in the intensity of imported intermediate inputs in the production of processing exports and that in other demand sources (for domestic final sales

Figure 2.9 Current Account Deficits, U.S. Unemployment, and the RMB-$ Exchange Rate

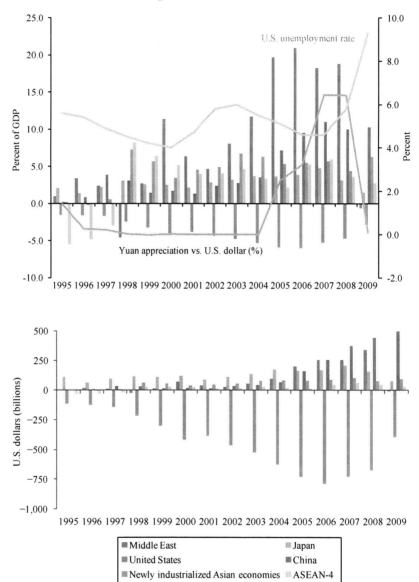

SOURCE: Author's calculations.

and normal exports). Since processing exports have accounted for more than 50 percent of China's exports every year at least since 1996, we felt that the HIY formula was likely to lead to a significant underestimation of the share of FVA in its exports. In fact, most economies offer tariff reductions or exemptions on imported intermediate inputs used in production for exports. By ignoring processing exports, one is likely to incorrectly estimate domestic and foreign content in trade, especially for economies that engage in a massive amount of tariff/tax-favored processing trade, such as China, Mexico, and Vietnam.

In Koopman, Wang, and Wei (2008; KWW in subsequent discussion), we aim to make two contributions to the literature. First, we present a formula for computing shares of foreign and domestic value added (DVA) in a country's exports when processing exports are pervasive. We develop this formula because we believe the production technology and input sourcing differs for goods produced for domestic consumption and normal exports compared to those produced under export processing regimes. We show that the HIY formula is a special case of this general formula. Second, we applied our methodology to China using data for 1997, 2002, and 2007. We estimate that the share of FVA in China's manufactured exports was about 50 percent in 1997–2002 before China's WTO membership—almost twice as high as that implied by the HIY formula—and has risen to over 60 percent in 2007 after five years of its WTO membership. Our method and data also allow us to examine sectoral level results, and we find interesting variations across sectors. Those sectors that are likely labeled as relatively sophisticated, such as computers, telecommunications equipment, and electronic devices, had particularly low domestic content (about 30 percent or less).

The approach in KWW is an accounting exercise and does not thoroughly examine the determinants, driving forces, and consequences of changes in domestic contents in China's gross exports. However, we believe we produced a solid methodology to estimate and account domestic and FVA in developing countries exports as a necessary first step toward a better understanding of these issues.

Besides HIY and related papers on vertical specialization, KWW is also related to the input-output (IO) literature. In particular, Chen et al. (2008) and Lau et al. (2007) are the first to develop a "noncompetitive" type IO model for China (i.e., one in which imported and domestically produced inputs are accounted for separately) and to incorporate processing exports explicitly. However, we believe that these papers do not describe a systematic way to infer separate IO coefficients for production of processing exports versus those for other final demands. As a result it is difficult for others to replicate their estimates or apply their methodologies to other countries. In addition, KWW use an aggregated version of China's 1995 and 2002 IO tables, respectively, to perform their analysis, with 20 some goods-producing industries. We provide a more up-to-date and more disaggregated assessment of FVA and DVA in Chinese exports with 83 goods-producing industries. Finally, they imposed an assumption in estimating the import use matrix from the competitive type IO table published by China's National Statistical Bureau: within each industry, the mix of the imported and domestic inputs is the same in capital formation, intermediate inputs, and final consumption. We relaxed this assumption by refining a method proposed in Dean, Fung, and Wang (2011) that combines China's processing imports statistics with the United Nations Broad Economic Categories classification.

The KWW Methodology

In this section we summarize the methodology developed in KWW. As the reader will see, the method is particularly innovative and generates very useful insights regarding domestic and foreign content of Chinese trade. This method has also been applied to Mexico's exports in De La Cruz et al. (2010), and more recently extended in a substantial way to examine global trade in value added in Koopman et al. (2010). In KWW we use very detailed information on China's trade regimes, bilateral and at the tariff line, to modify China's economy-wide IO data to reflect the substantial technology differences between its processing sectors and nonprocessing sectors. Our goal was to build on existing literature to split China's IO table into two parts, processing and nonprocessing, which would more accurately reflect the fact that the processing sector intensively used imported components that did not enter the domestic economy for other uses in final demand. Table 2.7 provides a sense of what we are trying to accomplish. We are essentially trying to estimate the values in the columns of the IO matrix for production for domestic use and normal exports and production of processing exports. A mathematical description of the approach follows.

Table 2.7 Input-Output Table with Separate Production Account for Processing Trade

		Intermediate use		Final use $(C+I+G+E)$	Gross output or imports
		Production for domestic use and normal exports	Production of processing exports		
	DIM	$1,2,\ldots,N$	$1,2,\ldots,N$	1	1
Domestic intermediate inputs	Production for domestic use and normal exports (D)	1 ⋮ N	Z^{DD}	Z^{DP}	$Y^D - E^P$	$X - E^P$
	Processing exports (P)	1 ⋮ N	0	0	E^P	E^P
Intermediate inputs from imports		1 ⋮ N	Z^{MD}	Z^{MP}	Y^M	M
Value-added		1	V^D	V^P		
Gross output		1	$X - E^P$	E^P		

SOURCE: Koopman, Wang, and Wei (2008).

We use superscript P and D, respectively, to represent processing exports and domestic sales and normal exports. This expanded IO model can be formally described by the following system of equations:

$$(2.1) \quad \begin{bmatrix} I - A^{DD} & -A^{DP} \\ 0 & I \end{bmatrix} \begin{bmatrix} X - E^P \\ E^P \end{bmatrix} = \begin{bmatrix} Y^D - E^P \\ E^P \end{bmatrix}$$

$$(2.2) \quad A^{MD}(X - E^P) + A^{MP} E^P + Y^M = M$$

$$(2.3) \quad uA^{DD} + uA^{MD} + A_v^D = u$$

$$(2.4) \quad uA^{DP} + uA^{MP} + A_v^P = u$$

The analytical solution of the system is

$$(2.5) \quad \begin{bmatrix} X - E^P \\ E^P \end{bmatrix} = \begin{bmatrix} I - A^{DD} & -A^{DP} \\ 0 & I \end{bmatrix}^{-1} \begin{bmatrix} Y^D - E^P \\ E^P \end{bmatrix}$$

The generalized Leontief inverse for this expanded model can be computed as follows:

$$(2.6) \quad B = \begin{bmatrix} I - A^{DD} & -A^{DP} \\ 0 & I \end{bmatrix}^{-1} = \begin{bmatrix} B^{DD} & B^{DP} \\ B^{PD} & B^{PP} \end{bmatrix} = \begin{bmatrix} I - A^{DD} & I - A^{DD} & A^{DP} \\ 0 & I \end{bmatrix}$$

$$= \begin{bmatrix} (I - A^{DD})^{-1} & (I - A^{DD})^{-1} A^{DP} \\ 0 & I \end{bmatrix}$$

Substituting Equation (2.6) into Equation (2.5), we have

$$(2.7) \quad X - E^P = (I - A^{DD})^{-1}(Y^D - E^P) + (1 - A^{DD})^{-1} A^{DP} E^P$$

Substituting Equation (2.7) into Equation (2.2), the total demand for imported intermediate inputs is

$$(2.8) \quad M - Y^M = A^{MD}(I - A^{DD})^{-1}(Y^D - E^P) + A^{MD}(1 - A^{DD})^{-1} A^{DP} E^P + A^{MP} E^P$$
$$+ A^{MP} E^P$$

It has three components: the first term is total imported content in final domestic sale and normal exports, and the second and third terms are indirect and direct imported content in processing exports, respectively.

We can compute vertical specialization (VS) or foreign content share in processing and normal exports in each industry separately:

$$(2.9) \quad \begin{vmatrix} VSS^D \\ VSS^P \end{vmatrix}^T = \begin{vmatrix} uA^{MD}(I-A^{DD})^{-1} \\ uA^{MD}(1-A^{DD})^{-1}A^{DP} + uA^{MP} \end{vmatrix}^T$$

The total foreign content share in a particular industry is the sum of the two weighted by the share of processing and nonprocessing exports s^P and $u-s^P$, where both s and u are a 1 by n vector:

$$(2.10) \quad \overline{VSS} = (u-s^P, s^P)\begin{vmatrix} VSS^D \\ VSS^P \end{vmatrix}$$

The foreign content (or FVA) share in a country's total exports is

$$(2.11) \quad TVSS = uA^{MD}(I-A^{DD})^{-1}\frac{E-E^P}{te} + (^{MD}(1-^{DD})^{-1}^{DP} + ^{MP})\frac{E^P}{te}$$
$$+ u(A^{MD}(1-A^{DD})^{-1}A^{DP} + A^{MP})\frac{E^P}{te}$$

where te is a scalar, the country's total exports. Equation (2.11) is a generalization of Equation (2.1), the formula to compute industry-level share of vertical specialization. Equation (2.11) is a generalization of the formula for country-level share of vertical specialization proposed by Hummels et al. (2001, p. 80). In particular, either when $A^{DD} = A^{DP}$ and $A^{MD} = A^{MP}$, or when $E^P/te = 0$, Equation (2.11) reduces to the HIY formula for VS.

Similarly, the domestic content share for processing and normal exports at the industry level can be computed separately:

$$(2.12) \quad \begin{vmatrix} DVS^D \\ DVS^P \end{vmatrix}^T = \bar{A}_v, B = (A_v^D \quad A_v^P)\begin{bmatrix} (I-A^{DD})^{-1} & (I-A^{DD})^{-1}A^{DP} \\ 0 & I \end{bmatrix}$$

$$= \begin{vmatrix} A_v^D(I-A^{DD})^{-1} \\ A_v^D(I-A^{DD})^{-1}A^{DP} + A_v^P \end{vmatrix}^T$$

The total domestic content share in a particular industry is a weighted sum of the two:

$$(2.13) \quad \overline{DVS} = (u - s^P, s^P) \begin{vmatrix} DVS^D \\ DVS^P \end{vmatrix}$$

The domestic content share in a country's total exports is

$$(2.14) \quad TDVS = A_V^D (I - A^{DD})^{-1} \frac{E - E^P}{te} + (\ _V^D (1 - \ ^{DD})^{-1} \ ^{DP} + \ _V^P) \frac{E^P}{te}$$

$$+ (A_V^D (1 - A^{DD})^{-1} A^{DP} + A_V^P) \frac{E^P}{te}$$

Either when $A^{DD} = A^{DP}$ and $A_v^D = A_v^P$ or when $E^P/te = 0$, Equation (2.14) reduces to the HIY formula. We can easily verify that for both processing and normal exports, the sum of domestic and foreign content shares is unity.

However, statistical agencies typically only report a traditional IO matrix, A^D, and sometimes A^M, but not A^{DP}, A^{DD}, A^{MP}, and A^{MD} separately. Therefore, a method to estimate these matrices, based on available information, had to be developed. In KWW we accomplish this through a quadratic programming model by combining information from trade statistics and conventional IO tables. The basic idea of this model is to use information from the standard IO table to determine sector-level total imports/exports, and information from trade statistics to determine the relative proportion of processing and normal exports within each sector, and thus use up all available data to split the national economy into processing and nonprocessing blocks, each with its own IO structure. Using the data from the IO table to determine sector-level total imports/exports helps to ensure that the balance conditions in the official IO account are always satisfied, and that the IO table with separate processing and nonprocessing accounts estimated from the model always sums to the published official table. Such a method is a formalization of the calibration methods widely used in macroeconomics and CGE modeling when the number of endogenous variables is larger than the number of equations (see KWW, pp. 9–14, for details of the method).

Estimation results

Table 2.8 presents the results from KWW for the decomposition of aggregate FVA and DVA shares in 1997, 2002, and 2007. For comparison, the results from the HIY method that ignores processing trade are also reported. The estimated aggregate DVA share in China's merchandise exports was 54 percent in 1997 and 60.6 percent in 2007. For manufacturing products, these estimated shares are slightly lower in levels but trending upward significantly at 50 percent in 1997 and 59.7 percent in 2007, respectively. In general, the estimated direct DVA shares are less than half of the total DVA shares. However, the estimated indirect FVA share was relatively small; most of the foreign content comes from directly imported foreign inputs, especially in 1997 and 2002. The indirect FVA increase over time and reach about a quarter of China's directly imported foreign inputs in 2007, indicating that the share of simple processing and assembling of foreign parts is declining, while more imported intermediates are being used in the production of other intermediate inputs that are then used in the production process.

Relative to the estimates from the HIY method, our procedure produces estimates of a much higher share of FVA in Chinese gross exports and with a different trend over time. To be more precise, estimates from the HIY method show that the foreign content share (total vs. share) increased steadily from 17.6 percent in 1997 to 28.7 percent in 2007 for all merchandise exports, and from 19.0 percent to 27.1 percent for manufacturing only during the same period. In contrast, our estimates

Table 2.8 Shares of Domestic and Foreign Value Added in Total Exports (%)

	The HIY method			The KWW method		
	1997	2002	2007	1997	2002	2007
All merchandise						
Total foreign value added	17.6	25.1	28.7	46.0	46.1	39.4
Direct foreign value added	8.9	14.7	13.7	44.4	42.5	31.6
Total domestic value added	82.4	74.9	71.3	54.0	53.9	60.6
Direct domestic value added	29.4	26.0	20.3	22.2	19.7	17.1
Manufacturing goods only						
Total foreign value added	19.0	26.4	27.1	50.0	48.7	40.3
Direct foreign value added	9.7	15.6	16.3	48.3	45.1	32.4
Total domestic value added	81.1	73.6	72.9	50.0	51.3	59.7
Direct domestic value added	27.5	24.6	24.6	19.6	18.1	16.5

SOURCE: Koopman, Wang, and Wei (2008).

suggest a trend in the opposite direction, with the share of FVA in all merchandise exports falling from 46 percent in 1997 to 39.4 percent in 2007, and a similar decline for the share in manufacturing exports, which fell from 50 percent in 1997 to 40.3 percent in 2007. The decline occurs mainly during the 2002–2007 period, which corresponds to the first five years of China's entry to the WTO. Our estimates indicate that the HIY method appears to incorrectly estimate both the level and the trend in domestic versus foreign content in the People's Republic of China exports.

What accounts for the difference between our and the HIY approaches? There are at least three factors that drive the change of foreign content of the country's gross exports: 1) the relative proportions of its total imports used as intermediate inputs in producing processing exports and domestic sales and normal exports; 2) the share of processing exports in its total exports; and 3) the sector composition of its exports. Because processing exports tend to use substantially more imported inputs, and processing exports account for a major share of China's total exports, the HIY indicator is likely to substantially underestimate the true foreign content in China's exports. This explains why the level of domestic content by our measure is much lower than that of the HIY indicator. On the other hand, as exporting firms (both those producing for normal exports and those for processing exports) gradually increase their intermediate inputs sourcing from firms within China, or multinationals move their upstream production to be near their downstream production, the extent of domestic content in exports rises over time. This is exactly what has happened since China joined the WTO. However, because exports from industries with relatively lower domestic content often grow faster due to dramatic inflow of foreign direct investment, the composition of a country's total exports may play as an offsetting factor to reduce the share of DVA in the country's gross exports and thus slow down the increase of DVA share in a country's total exports. As the Chinese government starts to reduce the policy incentives for both FIEs and processing exports at the end of 2006, we are observing a trend of increasing domestic contents in Chinese exports as China continues its industrial upgrading in the years to come.

Our interpretation is confirmed by DVA shares for processing and normal exports estimated separately (Table 2.9). There is a more than 10 percentage point increase in the total FVA share for domestic sales and normal exports between 1997 and 2007, which is consistent with the trend indicated by the HIY measure. However, in processing exports we see that more domestic-produced inputs were used, and DVA share increased from 20.7 percent in 1997 to 37.0 percent in 2007, up more than 16 percentage points. Because processing exports still constitute more than 50 percent of China's total exports in 2007 the weighted average total DVA share went up over the decade.

There are conflicting forces at work. On the one hand, as domestic input suppliers increase their quality over time, and multinationals move more and more of their upstream production into China, exporting firms may decide to increase local sourcing of their inputs. On the other hand, the reductions in the country's trade barriers also encourage exporting firms to use more imported inputs. These two opposing forces partially offset each other. However, on net, the domestic content share in China's exports appears to be on the rise. Looking ahead, the share of imported content in exports could fall or rise, depending on the relative speed with which domestic input suppliers and multinationals can step

Table 2.9 Domestic and Foreign Value Added: Processing vs. Normal Exports (% of total exports)

	Normal exports			Processing exports		
	1997	2002	2007	1997	2002	2007
All merchandise						
Total foreign value added	5.2	10.4	16.0	79.0	74.6	62.7
Direct foreign value added	2.0	4.2	5.0	78.6	73.0	58.0
Total domestic value added	94.8	89.6	84.0	21.0	25.4	37.3
Direct domestic value added	35.1	31.9	23.4	11.7	10.1	10.9
Manufacturing goods only						
Total foreign value added	5.5	11.0	16.4	79.4	75.2	63.0
Direct foreign value added	2.1	4.5	5.2	79.0	73.6	58.3
Total domestic value added	94.5	89.0	83.6	20.7	24.8	37.0
Direct domestic value added	31.5	29.5	22.4	11.7	10.0	10.9

SOURCE: Koopman, Wang, and Wei (2008) and author's estimates based on China's 1997, 2002, and 2007 benchmark input-output table published by the Bureau of National Statistics and Official China trade statistics from China Customs.

NOTE: The HIY method refers to estimates from using the approach in Hummels, Ishii, and Yi (2001). The KWW method refers to estimates from using the approach developed in this paper that takes into account special features of processing exports.

up their quality and variety versus the extent of additional reductions in the cost of using imported inputs.

Sectoral results

To see if there are interesting patterns at the sector level that help explain the decline trend of imported contents in China's total exports, and further assess whether the increasing DVA share reflects actual upgrade of Chinese industrial structure, Tables 2.10 and 2.11 report, in ascending order on domestic content share, the value-added decomposition in China manufacturing exports by industry in 2002 and 2007, respectively, together with shares of processing and foreign invested enterprises exports in each sector's exports as well as the sector's share in China's total merchandise exports. We choose to report the results from 2002 and 2007 not only because we would like to use the latest IO table released, but also because these two benchmark tables are consistently classified on most recent Chinese industry classifications, which simplifies issues involved in overtime comparison. Similar results for 1997 are omitted to save space.

Among the 57 manufacturing industries in Table 2.10, 15 have a share of DVA in their exports less than 50 percent in 2002, and collectively account for nearly 35 percent of China's merchandise exports that year. Many low-DVA industries are likely to be labeled as relatively sophisticated, such as telecommunications equipment, electronic computer, measuring instruments, and electronic devices. A common feature of these industries is that processing exports account for over two-thirds of their exports, and foreign-invested enterprises played an overwhelming role. In 2007, the number of industries with less than 50 percent domestic contents in their exports declined to 10, but their exports accounted for more than 32 percent of China's total merchandise exports, and these low-DVA industries are more concentrated in high-tech sectors. There are 11 industries in the top 15 low-DVA industries in 2002 that maintained that ranking in 2007.

The next 18 industries in Table 2.11 have their share of DVA in the range of 51–65 percent; they collectively accounted for 28 percent of China's total merchandise exports in 2002. Several labor-intensive sectors are in this group, such as furniture; toys and sports products; and leather, fur, and down products.

The remaining 24 industries have relatively high shares of DVA. However, as a group they produced less than 30 percent of China's total merchandise exports in 2002. Apparel, the country's largest labor-intensive exporting industry, which by itself was responsible for 7 percent of the country's total merchandise exports in 2002, is at the top of this group with a share of domestic content at 66 percent. The 12 industries at the bottom of Table 2.10 with DVA share more than 75 percent collectively produced only less than 10 percent of China's total merchandise exports in 2002.

The weights of high-DVA industries in China's exports increased significantly in 2007. The number of industries with a DVA share of more than 75 percent increased to 25 in 2007 (bottom of Table 2.11), and their exports constituted more than 30 percent of China's total merchandise exports in 2007. Among these high-DVA industries, we not only see the traditional labor industries such as furniture, textiles, and apparel still play a significant role (they account for more than half of these high-DVA-sector exports), but also the increasing role of heavy and capital-intensive industries such as automobile, industrial machinery, and rolling steel (they account for nearly one-third of these high-DVA sector's exports). The data clearly indicate China's industrial upgrade is real and FIEs have played a very important role in this process.

The groundbreaking work by HIY (2001) on vertical specialization needs to be interpreted with care, particularly in countries that make extensive use of processing trade. We find that for China the traditional HIY method substantially overestimated China's domestic content in its exports and underestimated foreign content in its exports as in Table 2.9. The HIY method estimates total DVA in Chinese exports ranging from 82 percent to 71 percent between 1997 and 2007, and that DVA was declining. The KWW method estimates that Chinese DVA ranged from 46 percent to 39 percent during this period, much lower than the HIY method, and that Chinese DVA was rising.

Further, with our method and data we could provide fairly detailed sectoral estimates of DVA in exports, as in Table 2.10. From this perspective you can observe that in 2002 China's DVA in telecommunications, shipbuilding, and electronic computers was less than 20 percent of exported value. Many high-tech or sophisticated exports contained

Table 2.10 Domestic Value-Added Share in Manufacturing Exports by Sector, 2002

| | Value-added decomposition (%) | | | | | | | | |
| | Nonprocessing | | Processing | | Weighted sum | | | | |
IO industry description	Foreign value added	Domestic value added	Foreign value added	Domestic value added	Foreign value added	Domestic value added	% of processing exports	% of FIE exports	% of FIE merchandise exports
Telecommunications equipment	12.6	87.5	94.7	5.3	87.5	12.5	91.2	88.4	3.2
Shipbuilding	17.7	82.3	85.3	14.7	82.5	17.5	95.8	21.0	0.6
Electronic computer	16.4	83.6	81.3	18.7	80.7	19.3	99.1	89.7	7.0
Cultural and office equipment	20.3	79.7	80.7	19.3	76.7	23.3	93.4	71.6	4.3
Household electric appliances	11.8	88.2	93.2	6.8	76.2	23.9	79.1	56.9	1.9
Household audiovisual apparatus	17.5	82.5	78.7	21.3	73.0	27.0	90.6	62.3	5.2
Printing, reproduction of recording media	8.9	91.1	80.3	19.7	68.1	31.9	83.0	62.7	0.3
Plastic	15.6	84.4	89.7	10.3	63.4	36.6	64.5	51.2	2.4
Electronic components	15.4	84.6	67.2	32.8	61.9	38.1	89.7	87.5	3.4
Steelmaking	11.0	89.0	87.2	12.8	55.8	44.3	58.8	86.1	0.0
Generators	14.8	85.2	68.1	32.0	55.7	44.3	76.8	55.8	0.9
Other electronic and communication equipment	2.2	97.8	64.0	36.0	54.7	45.3	84.9	84.9	1.8
Rubber	9.4	90.6	87.8	12.2	51.1	48.9	53.1	44.4	1.6
Nonferrous metal pressing	13.8	86.2	92.5	7.5	50.7	49.3	46.9	48.7	0.4
Measuring instruments	14.2	85.8	67.1	32.9	50.5	49.5	68.6	51.8	1.8
Paper and paper products	9.2	90.8	87.6	12.4	48.9	51.1	50.7	57.0	0.5
Furniture	11.7	88.3	87.5	12.5	47.5	52.5	47.2	56.8	1.7
Articles for culture, education, and sports activities	12.5	87.5	61.8	38.2	47.3	52.7	70.6	56.3	3.3

Nonferrous metal smelting	11.1	88.9	89.4	10.6	46.4	53.6	45.0	17.4	0.8
Smelting of ferroalloy	16.5	83.6	87.1	13.0	45.2	54.8	40.8	13.1	0.2
Synthetic materials	19.5	80.5	62.9	37.1	44.8	55.2	58.3	65.4	0.3
Petroleum refining and nuclear fuel	20.6	79.4	94.5	5.5	44.3	55.7	32.1	24.9	0.8
Metal products	9.7	90.3	89.8	10.2	44.3	55.7	43.2	45.6	4.4
Other transport equipment	14.0	86.0	87.3	12.7	44.2	55.8	41.2	50.5	1.2
Other electric machinery and equipment	11.6	88.4	59.9	40.1	43.9	56.2	66.8	60.1	5.6
Special chemical products	17.1	82.9	68.6	31.4	41.3	58.7	46.9	48.4	0.8
Other manufacturing products	10.8	89.2	68.7	31.3	41.0	59.0	52.2	37.6	1.7
Woolen textiles	8.9	91.1	91.2	8.8	40.0	60.1	37.8	42.6	0.3
Paints, printing inks, pigments, and similar products	16.5	83.5	91.7	8.3	38.4	61.6	29.1	44.4	0.4
Motor vehicles	10.5	89.6	90.0	10.0	38.4	61.6	35.2	48.2	0.8
Glass and its products	13.2	86.8	83.5	16.5	36.4	63.6	33.0	48.8	0.5
Leather, fur, down, and related products	8.1	91.9	59.7	40.4	36.1	63.9	54.3	50.3	4.5
Chemical products for daily use	14.7	85.3	73.2	26.8	36.0	64.1	36.3	43.6	0.4
Wearing apparel	8.7	91.3	65.7	34.3	34.4	65.6	45.1	39.2	7.0
Chemical fiber	19.8	80.2	90.8	9.2	34.3	65.7	20.5	29.2	0.0
Other special industrial equipment	10.8	89.3	68.0	32.0	33.6	66.4	39.9	44.0	1.3
Boilers, engines, and turbines	14.1	85.9	86.9	13.1	33.5	66.5	26.7	28.4	0.4
Other industrial machinery	9.9	90.1	61.4	38.6	32.4	67.6	43.7	43.7	3.5
Iron-smelting	13.2	86.8	89.0	11.0	31.2	68.8	23.7	3.0	0.1
Railroad transport equipment	16.2	83.9	85.4	14.6	29.9	70.1	19.9	5.9	0.1
Wood, bamboo, rattan, palm, and straw products	12.2	87.8	88.7	11.3	27.2	72.8	19.6	45.6	1.0

Table 2.10 (continued)

IO industry description	Value-added decomposition (%)						% of processing exports	% of FIE exports	% of merchandise exports
	Nonprocessing		Processing		Weighted sum				
	Foreign value added	Domestic value added	Foreign value added	Domestic value added	Foreign value added	Domestic value added			
Knitted and crocheted fabrics and articles	9.4	90.6	65.3	34.7	27.1	72.9	31.6	34.2	5.8
Agriculture, forestry, animal husbandry, and fishing machinery	14.3	85.7	86.1	13.9	27.1	72.9	17.8	20.8	0.1
Pesticides	23.0	77.0	88.5	11.5	27.1	72.9	6.3	14.4	0.2
Hemp textiles	10.5	89.5	88.3	11.7	25.7	74.3	19.5	19.5	0.3
Textiles productions	9.9	90.1	71.1	28.9	24.6	75.5	24.0	31.8	1.4
Cotton textiles	8.2	91.8	64.5	35.6	24.3	75.7	28.7	28.8	3.3
Fire-resistant materials	9.5	90.5	84.6	15.4	23.8	76.2	19.1	49.8	0.1
Metalworking machinery	12.8	87.2	81.2	18.8	21.9	78.1	13.3	27.0	0.2
Medicines	9.8	90.2	75.7	24.3	20.9	79.1	16.9	28.7	0.7
Pottery and porcelain	11.8	88.2	85.3	14.8	20.2	79.8	11.4	33.1	0.7
Other non-metallic mineral products	9.6	90.4	83.3	16.7	19.9	80.1	14.0	35.7	0.4
Fertilizers	15.6	84.4	90.3	9.7	18.9	81.1	4.5	21.7	0.1
Basic chemical raw materials	12.9	87.1	56.3	43.7	18.0	82.0	11.7	18.8	2.0
Rolling of steel	9.8	90.2	59.5	40.5	17.7	82.3	16.0	16.8	0.3
Cement, lime, and plaster	9.0	91.0	79.8	20.3	14.0	86.0	7.0	77.7	0.1
Coking	8.6	91.4	86.8	13.2	10.6	89.4	2.6	5.3	0.3
Total merchandise	10.4	89.6	74.6	25.4	46.1	53.9	55.7	51.8	92.5

SOURCE: Koopman, Wang, and Wei (2008). China 2002 and 2007 benchmark IO tables have 84 and 90 goods-producing sectors respectively; they both concord to China's 4 digit classification of economic activities (GB/T 4754-2002). This concordance enabled us to aggregate both year's estimates to 77 consistent goods-producing industries reported in this table.

less than 40 percent of Chinese domestic content. On the other hand, many of China's historical export sectors, such as apparel, textiles and fabrics, and many steel or metal-related items, had domestic content in excess of 60 percent. These estimates suggest that studies that examine extraordinary sophistication of China's exports, such as that by Rodrik (2006) and Schott (2008), might need to be interpreted with some care, as this sophistication may reflect the embodiment of sophisticated imported components. Further, if the domestic content in exports from China is low, especially in sectors that would have been considered sophisticated or high-skilled in the United States, then imports from the PRC may still generate a large downward pressure on the wage of the low-skilled Americans after all (as pointed out by Krugman [2008]). These are important policy questions and have implications for both developing and developed countries. A good understanding of the nature and extent of global supply chains could provide important insights for economists and policymakers.

The work we did on China, similar work for Mexico (De La Cruz et al. 2010), and a growing literature on value added in trade led us to develop a method to look at global value added trade, while incorporating the insights we developed for large single country traders making heavy use of processing. Thus, in Koopman et al. (2010) we develop an estimation technique designed to tie, at a global level, value-added estimates to gross trade flows, which is the most commonly available trade data and is heavily used to support various policy positions. Thus we use IO techniques to examine global value chain links using gross exports as a weighting mechanism. In this chapter we fully characterized value-added contributions from direct and indirect sources in a country's gross exports, formally generalizing the concept of vertical specialization to account for all sources of value added in gross exports in a multicountry, multisector framework. It also connects the vertical trade literature with value-added trade literature, generalizing concepts such as DVA that returns home in goods and services after being processed or finished abroad, denoted VS1* by Daudin, Rifflart, and Schweisguth (2009). This measure can be sizable for some large advanced economies.

To do this, we first divide gross exports into final demand and intermediates. Within intermediates, we further divide those goods that are consumed by the direct importer from those goods that are processed

Table 2.11 Domestic Value-Added Share in Manufacturing Exports by Sector, 2007

IO industry description	Value-added decomposition (%)						% of processing exports	% of FIE exports	% of merchandise exports
	Nonprocessing		Processing		Weighted sum				
	Foreign value added	Domestic value added	Foreign value added	Domestic value added	Foreign value added	Domestic value added			
Electronic component	22.5	77.5	76.9	23.1	67.7	32.3	83.1	89.8	4.9
Household audiovisual apparatus	24.1	75.9	70.4	29.6	67.4	32.6	93.4	79.1	2.5
Electronic computer	24.3	75.7	67.1	33.0	66.2	33.9	97.9	93.3	11.3
Cultural and office equipment	25.9	74.1	66.9	33.1	63.5	36.5	91.7	86.4	1.6
Other electronic and communication equip.	32.0	68.0	65.3	34.7	60.3	39.7	84.8	81.6	1.4
Telecommunications equipment	24.8	75.2	64.7	35.3	56.4	43.6	79.3	83.6	5.9
Shipbuilding	16.1	83.9	60.9	39.1	56.2	43.8	89.4	16.5	1.1
Petroleum refining and nuclear fuel	31.3	68.7	79.9	20.1	55.6	44.4	50.1	27.3	0.7
Measuring instruments	20.0	80.0	62.2	37.8	54.2	45.8	81.2	73.3	2.5
Synthetic materials	23.6	76.4	66.1	34.0	52.4	47.7	67.7	66.1	0.6
Household electric appliances	18.0	82.0	64.4	35.6	48.2	51.8	65.1	61.7	2.7
Other electric machinery and equipment	19.7	80.3	66.3	33.7	47.9	52.1	60.5	65.9	4.9
Rubber	18.3	81.8	73.0	27.0	46.7	53.4	51.8	41.9	1.7
Plastic	19.2	80.8	68.9	31.1	44.9	55.1	51.7	54.7	1.7
Articles for culture, education, and sports activities	17.0	83.0	54.4	45.6	41.7	58.4	66.0	64.9	2.1
Special chemical products	23.3	76.7	66.0	34.0	38.4	61.6	35.3	51.2	0.8
Chemical fiber	23.6	76.4	48.1	51.9	37.4	62.6	56.2	48.7	0.3
Other special industrial equipment	17.5	82.5	57.0	43.0	34.8	65.2	43.8	54.7	2.7

Generators	19.7	80.3	48.8	51.2	33.4	66.6	47.2	50.3	0.7
Railroad transport equipment	22.3	77.7	45.9	54.1	31.0	69.0	37.0	12.2	0.1
Leather, fur, down, and related products	9.6	90.4	59.6	40.4	30.8	69.2	42.5	46.0	2.4
Paper and paper products	14.5	85.5	42.4	57.6	30.8	69.2	58.4	62.8	0.4
Metal products	15.0	85.1	60.4	39.7	29.9	70.1	32.9	49.5	4.4
Boilers, engines, and turbines	18.4	81.6	61.3	38.7	29.4	70.6	25.6	37.8	0.5
Nonferrous metal pressing	21.4	78.6	43.9	56.1	28.8	71.2	32.7	41.4	1.0
Other manufacturing products	13.5	86.5	52.0	48.1	27.7	72.3	36.8	41.5	1.6
Paints, printing inks, pigments, and similar products	23.5	76.5	43.2	56.8	27.5	72.6	20.1	47.3	0.3
Pesticides	26.1	73.9	46.5	53.6	27.1	72.9	4.8	19.5	0.1
Chemical products for daily use	19.2	80.8	41.6	58.4	26.7	73.3	33.5	55.5	0.3
Nonferrous metal smelting	23.8	76.2	43.6	56.4	26.7	73.3	14.6	19.6	0.8
Other transport equipment	19.0	81.0	45.1	54.9	26.2	73.8	27.8	46.5	0.9
Basic chemical raw materials	19.2	80.8	57.5	42.5	25.1	74.9	15.6	26.4	1.9
Motor vehicles	16.0	84.0	52.6	47.4	24.7	75.3	23.7	42.0	2.0
Agriculture, forestry, animal husbandry, and fishing machinery	19.4	80.6	42.3	57.7	24.4	75.6	21.9	32.7	0.1
Other industrial machinery	16.5	83.6	43.8	56.2	24.4	75.6	29.0	49.9	3.4
Iron-smelting	24.1	75.9	49.4	50.6	24.4	75.6	1.1	24.3	0.1
Smelting of ferroalloy	24.3	75.7	46.7	53.3	24.4	75.6	0.4	8.8	0.4
Furniture	13.3	86.7	43.9	56.1	23.8	76.2	34.2	56.0	2.0
Printing, reproduction of recording media	13.6	86.4	39.0	61.0	23.5	76.5	39.0	44.4	0.2
Glass and its products	16.7	83.3	41.0	59.0	23.3	76.7	27.2	46.4	0.6
Woolen textiles	10.6	89.4	42.2	57.9	23.1	76.9	39.8	46.8	0.2

Table 2.11 (continued)

| | Value-added decomposition (%) | | | | | | | | |
| | Nonprocessing | | Processing | | Weighted sum | | | | |
IO industry description	Foreign value added	Domestic value added	Foreign value added	Domestic value added	Foreign value added	Domestic value added	% of processing exports	% of FIE exports	% of merchandise exports
Metalworking machinery	18.8	81.2	43.2	56.8	22.7	77.3	16.0	36.4	0.3
Rolling of steel	20.0	80.0	47.2	52.9	22.2	77.8	8.3	22.6	3.8
Fertilizers	19.0	81.0	42.7	57.3	22.1	77.9	13.2	9.5	0.3
Cotton textiles	12.0	88.0	54.3	45.8	21.1	78.9	21.5	26.1	2.1
Wearing apparel	10.5	89.5	46.1	53.9	21.0	79.0	29.7	36.9	4.6
Medicines	12.4	87.6	62.5	37.5	19.7	80.3	14.5	32.3	0.8
Wood, bamboo, rattan, palm, and straw products	15.4	84.6	41.7	58.4	19.6	80.4	16.1	33.1	1.0
Steelmaking	19.2	80.8	48.3	51.7	19.2	80.8	0.2	7.1	0.3
Pottery and porcelain	16.6	83.4	41.9	58.2	18.0	82.0	5.2	29.9	0.5
Textiles productions	11.6	88.4	45.1	54.9	17.6	82.4	18.1	35.1	1.8
Knitted and crocheted fabrics and articles	11.8	88.2	48.4	51.6	17.5	82.5	15.6	25.7	5.7
Other non-metallic mineral products	14.0	86.0	43.4	56.6	17.0	83.0	10.1	25.1	0.5
Hemp textiles	13.4	86.6	43.2	56.8	16.1	83.9	9.0	14.7	0.2
Fire-resistant materials	13.5	86.6	44.9	55.1	15.3	84.7	5.8	51.6	0.1
Cement, lime, and plaster	11.0	89.0	47.1	52.9	11.6	88.4	1.7	29.6	0.1
Coking	10.4	89.6			10.4	89.6	0.0	11.4	0.3
Total merchandise	16.0	84.0	62.7	37.3	39.4	60.6	50.1	55.7	96.0

SOURCE: Author's calculations. China 2002 and 2007 benchmark IO tables have 84 and 90 goods-producing sector, respectively; they both concord to China's 4 digit classification of economic activities (GB/T 4754–2002). This concordance enables us to aggregate both years' estimates to 77 consistent goods-producing industries reported in this table.

and exported by the direct importer for consumption or further processing in a third country:

$$(2.15) \quad E_{rs} = Y_{rs} + A_{rs}X_s = \underbrace{\quad}_{rs} + \underbrace{\quad}_{rs\ ss} + \underbrace{\quad}_{rs\ st} + \underbrace{\quad}_{rs}$$

$$\underbrace{Y_{rs}}_{\substack{\text{Final goods} \\ \text{exported to } s}} + \underbrace{A_{rs}X_{ss}}_{\substack{\text{Intermediates} \\ \text{absorbed in } s}} + \underbrace{\sum_{t\neq r,s} A_{rs}X_{st}}_{\substack{\text{Processed and exported} \\ \text{to third countries}}} + \underbrace{A_{rs}X_{sr}}_{\substack{\text{Processed and} \\ \text{exported back to } r}}$$

where X_{st} is the output of country s used to produce goods absorbed in country t. Note that the last three terms sum to the bilateral gross trade in intermediate goods, and each may include both intermediates and final products produced in the importing country s.

In Koopman et al. (2010), we transform the above equation to arrive at our key decomposition equation that states that a country's gross exports to the world is the sum of the following five broad terms:

$$(2.16) \quad E_{r*} = DV_r + FV_r$$

$$= \underbrace{V_r B_{rr} \sum_{s\neq r} Y_{rs}}_{(1)} + \underbrace{V_r B_{rr} \sum_{s\neq r} A_{rs}X_{ss}}_{(2)} + \underbrace{V_r B_{rr} \sum_{s\neq r}\sum_{t\neq r,s} A_{rs}X_{st}}_{(3)} + \underbrace{V_r B_{rr} \sum_{s\neq r} A_{rs}X_{sr}}_{(4)} +$$

$$\underbrace{+ V_r B_{rr} \sum_{s\neq r} A_{rs}X_{sr}}_{(4)} + \underbrace{FV_r}_{(5)}$$

where,

(1) DVA embodied in exports of final goods and services absorbed by the direct importer,

(2) DVA embodied in exports of intermediate inputs used by the direct importer to produce its domestically needed products,

(3) DVA embodied in intermediate exports used by the direct importer to produce goods for third countries (indirect value-added exports),

(4) DVA embodied in intermediate exports used by the direct importer to produce goods shipped back to source (reflected DVA), and

(5) value added from foreign countries embodied in gross exports (FVA used in exports).

This decomposition formula is also shown in Figure 2.10, which integrates the older literature on vertical specialization with the newer literature on value-added trade, while ensuring that measured value added from all sources accounts for total gross exports. The vertical specialization literature emphasized that gross exports contain two sources of value added, domestic and foreign. The second equation above shows that a country's DVA could be further broken down into additional components that reveal the destination of a country's exported value added, including its own value added that returns home in its imports.[9] The sum of (1), (2), and (3) equals each country's value-added exports to the world; the sum of (1), (2), (3), and (4) equals domestic content in a country's gross exports, thus nicely connecting the two major concepts in the vertical specialization and value-added trade literature on the one hand, and clearly distinguishing them on the other hand.

In addition, all other measures in the literature can be derived from a combination of the five basic measures. For instance, the sum of (3) and (4) equals HIY's VS1 in gross exports; the sum of (1), (2), and (3) divided by gross exports equals Johnson and Noguera's (2010) ratio of value-added exports to gross exports (VAX ratio); and the sum of (4) and (5) equals the portion of trade that is double counted in official trade statistics.[10]

In Table 2.12 we report the global decomposition by country or regional grouping in our database for 2004 and map it back to the existing measures in the literature. An interesting insight reported in the table is our estimate of the double or multiple counting (column 9) in global trade flows as a result of value added moving across multiple borders. We estimate that the global average is 25.6 percent. One can observe a number of interesting insights from this global approach. We can see that some countries, such as Japan, Indonesia, and the Philippines, are important intermediate suppliers, providing indirect value added through their exports to third countries. Some countries such as Brazil, Russia, Canada, Australia, and New Zealand export a lot of value-added intermediates that are consumed by the direct importer. Another interesting insight is that the EU and the United States have a much greater share of their DVA exports return home to them embedded in other countries' exports.

Figure 2.10 Decomposition of Gross Exports: Concepts

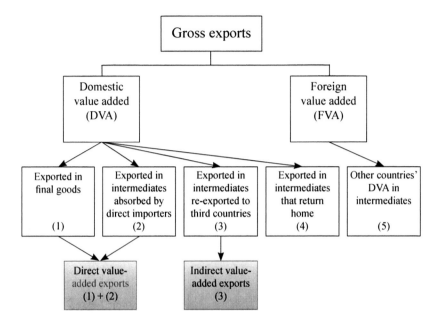

NOTE: (4) is also labeled as VS1* by Daudin et al. (2009). (5) is labeled as VS, and (3) + (4) is labeled as VS1 by HIY (2001). (4) and (5) involve value added that crosses national borders at least twice, and are the sources of multiple counting of value added in standard trade statistics. The share of domestic content in a country's exports equals (1) + (2) + (3) + (4). (1) + (2) is the VAX ratio for each country's exports to the world defined by Johnson and Noguera (2010).
SOURCE: Koopman et al. (2010).

This global approach also allows us to provide interesting policy-relevant insights that otherwise might not have been evident. For example, in the USITC's recent study (2011) we provide insights on U.S. trade using value-added trade data.[11] Although U.S. imports from China and Mexico are considerable, these countries contribute less value added to U.S. imports than Europe, Canada, and Japan, the three largest contributors to value added (Table 2.13). Remarkably, U.S. value added that returns home after receiving further processing elsewhere ranks fourth, at 8.3 percent. Among all countries, the United States has the highest share of its own value-added exports returned home in its

Table 2.12 Decomposition of Gross Exports, 2004

	Basic decomposition					Connection with existing measures				
	DVA in direct exports of final goods	DVA in intermediates absorbed by direct importer	Indirect DVA exports to third countries	Retuned DVA	Foreign value added	VAX ratio[a]	VS1[b]	Domestic content[b]	Multiple counting	GVC participation (vertical trade, OECD)
	(1)	(2)	(3)	(4)	(5)	(6)	(7)	(8)	(9)	(10)
Advanced economies										
Australia, New Zealand	27.0	33.6	27.4	0.6	11.5	88.0	27.9	88.5	12.0	39.4
Canada	23.5	36.2	10.9	1.3	28.1	70.5	12.2	71.9	29.5	40.4
EFTA	23.0	36.3	14.7	0.8	25.2	74.0	15.5	74.8	26.0	40.8
EU	38.1	29.6	13.5	7.4	11.4	81.1	20.9	88.6	18.9	32.3
Japan	38.4	18.5	28.0	2.9	12.2	84.9	30.8	87.8	15.1	43.1
United States	32.5	27.6	14.6	12.4	12.9	74.6	27.0	87.1	25.4	39.9
Asian NICs										
Hong Kong	27.2	25.8	18.9	0.6	27.5	71.9	19.5	72.5	28.1	47.0
Korea	29.5	13.5	22.3	0.9	33.9	65.2	23.2	66.1	34.8	57.0
Taiwan	19.2	12.6	26.4	0.8	41.1	58.2	27.1	58.9	41.8	68.2
Singapore	11.0	13.1	12.2	0.6	63.2	36.3	12.8	36.8	63.7	76.0
Emerging Asia										
China normal	44.2	20.3	19.7	1.2	14.6	84.2	20.9	85.4	15.8	35.5
China processing	28.8	10.2	4.1	0.3	56.6	43.1	4.4	43.4	56.9	61.0
Indonesia	20.0	28.1	28.4	0.6	22.9	76.5	29.0	77.1	23.5	51.9
Malaysia	16.7	17.7	24.1	0.9	40.5	58.6	25.0	59.5	41.4	65.5

Philippines	17.6	11.1	29.0	0.4	41.9	57.8	29.4	58.1	42.2	71.2
Thailand	27.9	14.0	18.1	0.3	39.7	60.0	18.5	60.3	40.0	58.1
Vietnam	32.9	15.3	14.4	0.4	37.0	62.6	14.8	63.0	37.4	51.8
Rest of East Asia	35.3	26.9	16.1	0.1	21.7	78.2	16.2	78.3	21.8	37.9
India	30.2	30.8	18.6	0.4	20.1	79.6	18.9	79.9	20.4	39.0
Rest of South Asia	48.8	19.2	10.6	0.1	21.3	78.6	10.7	78.7	21.4	32.0
Other emerging										
Brazil	27.4	40.7	19.0	0.3	12.7	87.0	19.2	87.3	13.0	31.9
EU accession countries	28.7	29.2	10.4	1.0	30.8	68.3	11.4	69.2	31.7	42.1
Mexico normal	23.5	41.1	17.4	0.6	17.3	82.1	18.1	82.7	17.9	35.3
Mexico processing	20.6	10.1	5.6	0.3	63.4	36.3	5.9	36.7	63.7	69.3
Rest of Americas	23.8	40.6	20.4	0.7	14.4	84.9	21.2	85.6	15.2	35.6
Russian Federation	9.5	49.1	30.5	0.7	10.2	89.1	31.2	89.8	10.9	41.4
South Africa	23.1	34.5	24.0	0.2	18.2	81.6	24.2	81.8	18.4	42.4
Rest of the world	15.0	45.6	22.4	2.5	14.6	83.0	24.9	85.4	17.0	39.5
World average	29.2	27.7	17.5	4.0	21.5	74.4	21.5	78.5	25.6	43.0

[a] Data from Johnson and Noguera (2010).
[b] Data from Hummels, Ishii, and Yi (2001).
NOTE: All columns are expressed as a share of total gross exports. DVA = domestic value added. Country groupings follow IMF regions (http://www.imf.org/external/pubs/ft/weo/2010/01/weodata/groups.htm#oem).
SOURCE: Author's calculations.

imports.[12] This high share reflects both the large size of the U.S. market and its tight integration with Canada and Mexico.

The value-added approach more accurately portrays the origin of the value in U.S. imports than can standard gross import data. For example, Japan has an 8.7 percent share of total U.S. imports, but accounts for 10.4 percent of the value added in U.S. imports. Japan's higher share of value-added imports indicates that a substantial share of its exports (26 percent) first journey to other countries and undergo additional processing before being exported to the United States. Specifically, Japan produces a large volume of high-value components that are shipped to other Asian countries, particularly China, where they are assembled into consumer goods and then exported (Dean, Lovely, and Mora 2009). In contrast, China's share of U.S. value-added imports (7.7 percent) is less than its share of total U.S. imports (11.1 percent). China is the final assembler in a number of supply chains in which Japan and other countries in East Asia supply parts. Similarly, exports from many smaller East Asian countries pass through third countries, such as China, before entering the United States. Canada and Mexico also have lower shares of U.S. value-added imports than their total U.S. imports. U.S. imports from Canada and Mexico contain many U.S.-produced components, which contribute to the large share of U.S. exported value that returns home. Obviously understanding the underlying geographic composition of value added in imports can ensure a deeper understanding of a large number of policy issues, such as FTA negotiations, supply chain disruptions, and the impact of currency revaluations.

Various countries and regions contribute value to U.S. imports in different sectors (Table 2.14). Europe is the largest source of value added for many sectors, particularly business services. U.S.-returned value added is most significant in motor vehicles and parts (19.1 percent); much of this represents value added returned home from other NAFTA countries, as the United States is heavily involved in auto supply chains in this region. Europe and Japan also contribute significant amounts of value added to U.S. imports of motor vehicles and parts. U.S.-returned value added is also fairly high for apparel (11.0 percent), since some rules of origin provide for duty-free imports of apparel made from U.S. yarns and fabrics. East Asia, which has abundant low-cost labor and is well integrated into supply chains with China, contributed the most value added to U.S. imports of apparel (27.8 percent).[13]

Table 2.13 U.S. Imports and Value-Added Shares in U.S. Imports, 2004, by Source

Region	Total imports ($, millions)	Share of general imports (%)	Share of value-added imports (%)	Share of value-added passing through a third country before entering the United States (%)
Europe	393,301	24.7	26.1	17.6
Canada	242,170	15.2	11.0	3.2
Japan	138,417	8.7	10.4	26.0
United States	—	0.0	8.3	100.0
China	176,879	11.1	7.7	14.8
Mexico	154,571	9.7	4.9	4.0
Rest of Americas[a]	76,183	4.8	4.7	13.2
Developing East Asia	79,250	5.0	4.5	32.4
Taiwan, Singapore, Hong Kong	73,066	4.6	4.3	36.7
Korea	51,707	3.3	3.3	31.8
Brazil	23,662	1.5	1.6	20.3
Australia and New Zealand	15,717	1.0	1.3	33.6
Russia	12,003	0.8	1.3	46.4
India	17,486	1.1	1.1	22.0
South Asia	9,557	0.6	0.5	10.2
Rest of world	120,320	7.6	8.5	23.5
Total	1,590,124	100.0	100.0	25.8[b]

[a]Including South American, Central American, and Caribbean countries other than Mexico and Brazil.
[b]U.S. average, weighted by U.S. imports from all sources.
SOURCE: Commission estimates. Table 3.2 in the USITC study.

Table 2.14 Country or Regional Sources of Value Added on U.S. Imports, Selected Sectors, 2004 (%)

Sector	U.S returned	China	Japan	East Asia	Canada	Mexico	Latin America	Europe	Others
Total	8.3	7.7	10.4	12.0	11.0	4.9	6.3	26.1	13.2
Selected sectors									
Apparel	11.0	11.2	2.4	27.8	2.4	2.0	10.4	11.4	21.4
Chemicals, rubber, and plastics	6.3	5.0	9.7	8.7	12.0	2.5	3.6	42.8	9.4
Motor vehicles and parts	19.1	2.5	23.0	7.2	16.0	3.8	1.9	23.1	3.4
Electronic equipment	8.6	14.4	19.0	29.6	2.4	9.3	1.3	11.4	3.9
Machinery and equipment	11.3	10.1	17.2	9.7	6.9	4.7	2.9	32.1	5.1
Business services	1.5	1.3	6.2	12.7	8.8	0.2	2.7	55.5	11.3

SOURCE: Commission estimates from USITC (2008, Table 3.3).

Sectoral insights on value-added imports can again inform FTA negotiations, provide insights on supply chain disruptions, and help identify
potential indirect effects of protection measures.

The value-added shares of U.S. absorption (i.e., the use of intermediate inputs plus consumption of final products, or equivalently total
domestic expenditures on goods and services) provide another view of
the sectors and regions where global value chains are important to the
U.S. economy. Absorption can distinguish the relative U.S. and FVA
shares in products consumed in the United States. Overall, the United
States itself generates a large share (89 percent) of the value of final and
intermediate goods that it uses (Table 2.15). This share is on par with
those of Japan (90 percent) and the EU-15 (88 percent), and is higher
than those of most developing countries.[14] The many goods and services produced and consumed in the United States and the large portion
of U.S. value returned in imports contribute to the high share.

Although overall U.S. value in absorption is high, the domestic
value share is typically lower for sectors actively involved in global
supply chains. There is substantial foreign content in electronic equipment, apparel, and motor vehicles. For apparel, consistent with value
added in imports, China and East Asia contribute more value to U.S.
absorption than Mexico and Latin America (largely from Central America). Japan, Canada, and Europe are major participants in supply chains
for motor vehicles and parts, and together account for almost one-third
of the value added in U.S. absorption in the sector. Japan, East Asia,
Mexico, and Europe participate in the supply chain for electronic equipment, which is one of the largest in terms of the number of countries
contributing significant value added. Electronics has the highest share
of foreign content: fully two-thirds of the value of all electronics products used by U.S. industry and consumers originates abroad. Hence,
foreign value in some U.S. industries may be substantially higher than
estimates in previous studies based on gross input use or gross trade.

In business services, a category that includes consulting and computer support, the United States provides a large portion (88.5 percent)
of its absorbed value added, while Europe contributes 5.9 percent.
Despite the high profile of India's consulting and computer services
and the prominence of some large suppliers, India supplied only 0.1
percent of the value added in U.S. absorption of business services in
2004, though this may have risen in recent years.

Table 2.15 Country or Regional Sources of Value Added in U.S. Absorption, Selected Sectors, 2004 (%)

Sector	U.S.	China	Japan	East Asia	Canada	Mexico	Latin America	Europe	Others
Total	89.0	0.9	1.3	1.5	1.3	0.6	0.7	3.2	1.4
Selected sectors									
Apparel	54.3	4.1	0.6	18.3	2.1	1.8	5.7	2.9	8.6
Chemicals, rubber, and plastics	69.1	3.1	4.2	4.2	3.4	0.8	1.4	11.9	1.5
Motor vehicles and parts	57.3	1.5	11.3	3.4	10.1	4.6	0.6	10.6	0.5
Electronic equipment	33.3	9.3	12.7	23.3	1.8	10.9	0.8	7.0	0.8
Machinery and equipment	76.1	2.7	4.5	3.1	2.2	1.6	0.7	8.4	0.6
Business services	88.5	0.3	1.4	1.1	1.4	0.0	0.5	5.9	0.8

SOURCE: Commission estimates from USITC (2008, Table 3.4).

In addition, the U.S. trade balance is a frequently discussed trade issue. The United States has had large trade deficits in recent years (e.g., $500 billion in 2010), and it has also had substantial bilateral deficits with major trading partners. The value-added trade work discussed here, and in the literature more broadly, has demonstrated that many countries may add value to a particular good or service in a global supply chain, and that attributing the entire export value to the last exporting country can provide a misleading picture of the sources of value in trade. While the overall trade balance is not affected by value-added calculations, examinations of bilateral trade balances on a value-added basis yield different conclusions about the extent to which specific foreign countries contribute to a country's deficit, and here we will focus on the U.S. deficit.

The contribution of China to the U.S. trade deficit differs substantially depending on which of the two measures is used. China is often the final assembler in a large number of global supply chains, and it uses components from many other countries to produce its exports. In Figure 2.11 we see that the U.S.-China trade deficit on a value-added basis is considerably smaller (by about 40 percent in 2004) than on the commonly reported basis of official gross trade.[15] In contrast, Japan exports parts and components to countries throughout Asia, many of which are eventually assembled into final products and exported to the United States. Thus the U.S.-Japan trade balance on a value-added basis is larger than the comparable gross trade deficit. The U.S. value-added trade deficits with other major trading partners (Canada, Mexico, and the EU-15) differ by smaller amounts from their corresponding gross trade deficits.

There is significant political debate in the United States regarding efforts to encourage China to appreciate the Renminbi (RMB) faster. The logic behind this argument is that if the RMB were to unilaterally appreciate by 30 percent, then Chinese export prices will increase by 30 percent, raising prices in the United States of Chinese products and reducing U.S. demand for those imported products. Apparently expectations are that U.S. consumers would then buy other, U.S-made products, or production of those products would shift back to the United States, and/or U.S. consumers would decide to save the money they otherwise would have spent, resulting in an overall decline in U.S. imports. Furthermore, a number of commentators have suggested that such an

Figure 2.11 U.S. Bilateral Trade Deficits with Major Trading Partners, 2004

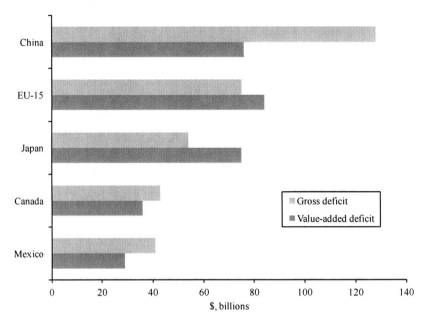

SOURCE: Commission estimates from USITC (2008, box 3.4)

appreciation could raise U.S. employment anywhere from 600,000 to 2.3 million additional jobs.[16]

However, unilateral RMB appreciation will likely raise the costs of Chinese content, or value added, in its exports. Thus, if Chinese value added for electronics products is 15 percent of its exports prices, then a 30 percent appreciation of the RMB could raise the price of Chinese electronics products by only 4.5 percent, not 30 percent. Of course, historically, exchange rate pass through has typically been much less than 1.0, perhaps because of value-added content related issues, but also because of competitive pricing decisions by exporters who may absorb some of the increase. Further, it appears more likely that U.S. consumers would continue to demand similar products, probably imported from some other international supplier, at a higher price, though perhaps priced in a different currency. An excellent overview of these issues can be found in Arnold (2008). Thus, with a more in-depth understanding of value-added trade, one can better understand the potential impact on country-specific export prices based on a currency appreciation.

Another insight gained from value-added trade is correcting a fairly standard, though potentially misleading, measure of export's contribution to GDP growth. In Figure 2.12 we see that export growth as a share of GDP is not necessarily a good indicator of GDP growth, as Mexico, a country with a relatively high ratio of export to GDP, has had mixed GDP growth over the period, while countries such as Brazil and India, with relatively low shares of export to GDP growth, are experiencing rather robust and extensive economic growth. McKinsey researchers illustrated that export growth's contribution to economic growth in China using traditional GDP growth decomposition methods was very misleading (Horn, Singer, and Woetzel 2010). Using traditional methods suggests that exports contributed 40–60 percent of China's economic growth from 1990 to 2008; however, they recalculate China's GDP growth for 2002–2007, 2008, and 2009, adopt the KWW (2008) method, and find that exports contributed 14–27 percent of overall GDP

Figure 2.12 Gross Exports as a Share of GDP, Selected Countries

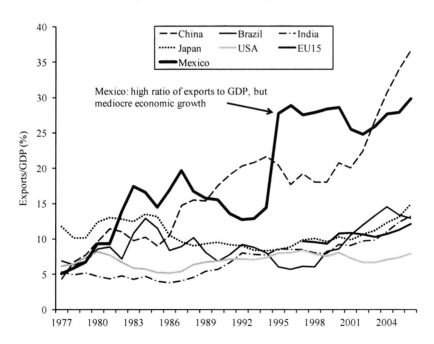

growth and that the role of investment and private consumption are substantially more important. Economists generally view sustained economic growth as being driven by investment and consumption growth on the demand side.

In sum, the fact that we can now generate single country and global value-added trade databases now allows the insights generated from a vast array of product-specific value and supply chain case studies to be translated into more aggregated data tied to traditional measures of global trade. The ability to combine product level case studies with sector and country level data is a major step forward in our efforts to more accurately inform policymakers about the impacts and implications of trade and trade policy.

Notes

The contributions of Zhi Wang, Shang-Jin Wei, and Justino De La Cruz are greatly appreciated; however, any and all remaining errors in this paper are mine. The views expressed here are solely those of the author and do not reflect the views of the U.S. International Trade Commission or any of its commissioners.

1. For a more extensive discussion on these issues see, for example, Fosler and Bottelier (2007) and Branstetter and Lardy (2006).
2. Ahearne et al. (2007) presents a nice summary.
3. See Hammer (2006) for extensive discussions on driving factors in U.S-China trade and Yao (2008) for a similar discussion on trade between China and the world.
4. This section is drawn from U.S. Trade Shifts found at http://www.usitc.gov/ tradeshifts/2007/default.htm (accessed June 27, 2012).
5. This is a very abbreviated summary of the U.S.-China trade relationship. For more detailed discussions of U.S.-China and China-world trade patterns, see Hammer (2006) and Yao (2008).
6. See, for example, testimony from C. Fred Bergsten, of the Peterson Institute of International Economics, before the Hearing on China's Exchange Rate Policy, Committee on Ways and Means, U.S. House of Representatives, September 15, 2012. http://waysandmeans.house.gov/media/transcript/9854.html#trumka (accessed June 27, 2012).
7. China's trade-weighted tariff rate reflects the relatively high tariffs remaining on imports of textiles and apparel. In fact, China's declining average tariff rate over the period in the table reflects more of the changing composition of China's exports increasingly toward products in lower tariff lines as found in HS 84.
8. De La Cruz et al. (2010); Koopman, Wang, and Wei (2010); and Powers et al. (2010) are among some of the papers generated from this effort. In the following

discussions on value-added trade in China and for global value added estimates, I draw heavily from sections of Koopman, Wang, and Wei (2008) and Koopman et al. (2010).

9. Since Equation (16) decomposes all bilateral exports from country s to country r, it also simultaneously decomposes bilateral imports.

10. Component (3) should not be included in double counting because when this value crosses a border the second time, it becomes foreign value in the direct importer's exports. For this reason, it is not included as double counting to avoid an overcorrection.

11. The discussion surrounding Tables 2.12, 2.13, and 2.14 draws heavily on USITC (2011).

12. The world average is 4.0 percent. Other economies with high shares include the EU (7.2 percent) and Japan (3.4 percent) (Koopman et al. 2010).

13. Major changes have occurred in global supply chains involving textiles and apparel since 2004, and China's prominence in U.S. imports has likely increased.

14. EU-15 refers to the first 15 countries to join the EU. DVA shares for Japan, the EU-15, and other countries come from Koopman et al. (2010).

15. Using a slightly different method, a recent study by the WTO and the Institute of Developing Economies–Japan External Trade Organization (2011) finds that this discrepancy was about 53 percent in 2005 and 42 percent in 2008. Johnson and Noguera (2010) have roughly similar results also, though in their estimates the bilateral U.S. deficit with Mexico reversed to a surplus.

16. Bergsten (2010) estimates between 600,000 and 1.2 million jobs from a substantial appreciation, Krugman (2010) estimates the effect at 1.4 million jobs, and Scott (2010) estimates 2.3 million jobs with a return of the bilateral deficit to 2001 levels. It has been difficult to reproduce employment impacts like this using standard USITC general equilibrium models, even when we restrict the model to force substitution of forgone imports to U.S. production.

References

Ahearne, Alan, William R. Cline, Kyung Tae Lee, Yung Chul Park, Jean Pisani-Ferry, and John Williamson. 2007. "Global Imbalances: Time for Action." PB07-4. Washington, DC: Peterson Institute for International Economics.

Arnold, Bruce. 2008. "How Changes in the Value of the Chinese Currency Affect U.S. Imports." CBO paper. Washington, DC: Congressional Budget Office.

Bems, Rudolf, Robert Johnson, and Kei-Mu Yi. 2009. "The Collapse of Global Trade: Update on the Role of Vertical Linkages." In *The Great Trade Collapse: Causes, Consequences and Prospects*, Richard Baldwin, ed. London: Centre for Economic Policy Research, pp. 79–86.

Bergsten, C. Fred. 2010. "Correcting the Chinese Exchange Rate: Testimony before Correcting the Hearing on China's Exchange Rate Policy: Committee on Ways and Means, U.S. House of Representatives." *Speeches, Testimony Papers*. Washington, DC: Peterson Institute for International Economics.   http://www.piie.com/publications/pubs_year.cfm?ResearchTypeID= 7&ResearchYear=2010 (accessed January 17, 2012).

Blonigen, B., and T.J. Prusa. 2003. "Anti-dumping." In *Handbook of International Trade*, E.K. Choi and J. Harrigan, eds. Oxford, U.K., and Cambridge, MA: Blackwell Publishers, pp. 251–284.

Branstetter, Lee, and Nicholas Lardy. 2006. "China's Emergence of Globalization." NBER Working Paper No. 12373. Cambridge, MA: National Bureau of Economic Research.

Chen, X., L. Cheng, K.C. Fung, and L.J. Lau. 2008. "The Estimation of Domestic Value-Added and Employment Induced by Exports: An Application to Chinese Exports to the US." In *China and Asia: Economic and Financial Interactions*, Y. Cheung and K. Wong, eds. Oxford: Routledge, pp. 64–82.

China Daily. 2007a. "Trade Dispute Unlikely to Spark Sino-U.S. Trade War." February 7. http://www.china.org.cn/international/opinion/2007-02/07/content_1199270.htm (accessed January 17, 2012).

———. 2007b. "Say No to Protectionism." February 13. http://www.china .org.cn/english/international/199980.htm (accessed January 17, 2012).

China State Council. 2005. "China's Peaceful Development Road." White paper. December 22. Beijing: China State Council Information Office. http://www.china.org.cn/english/2005/Dec/152669.htm#5 (accessed January 17, 2012).

Daudin, Guillaume, Christine Rifflart, and Danielle Schweisguth. 2009. "Who Produces for Whom in the World Economy?" Sciences Po (OFCE) Working Paper 2009-18. Paris: OFCE.

De La Cruz, Justino, Robert Koopman, Zhi Wang, and Shang-Jin Wei. 2010. "Estimating Foreign Value-Added in Mexico's Manufacturing Exports." USITC Working Paper. Washington, DC: U.S. International Trade Commission.

Dean, Judith, K. Fung, and Zhi Wang. 2011. "Measuring Vertical Specialization: The Case of China." *Review of International Economics* 19(4): 609–625.

Dean, Judith, Mary Lovely, and Jesse Mora. 2009. "Decomposing China-Japan-U.S. Trade: Vertical Specialization, Ownership, and Organizational Form." *Journal of Asian Economics* 20(6): 596–610.

Ferrantino, Michael, Zhi Wang, Robert Koopman, and Falan Yinug. 2010. "The Nature of U.S.-China Trade in Advanced Technology Products." *Comparative Economic Studies* 52(2): 207–224.

Fosler, Gail D., and Pieter Bottelier. 2007. *Can China's Growth Trajectory Be Sustained?* R-1410-07-RR. Washington, DC: Conference Board.

Hammer, Alexander. 2006. "The Dynamic Structure of U.S.-China Trade, 1995–2004." USITC Office of Economics Working Paper No. 2006-07-A. Washington, DC: U.S. International Trade Commission.

Horn, John, Vivien Singer, and Jonathan Woetzel. 2010. "A Truer Picture of China's Export Machine." *McKinsey Quarterly*, September. https://www .mckinseyquarterly.com/A_truer_picture_of_Chinas_export_machine_2676 (accessed July 17, 2012).

Hummels, David, Jun Ishii, and Kei-Mu Yi. 2001. "The Nature and Growth of Vertical Specialization in World Trade." *Journal of International Economics* 54(1): 75–96.

Irwin, Douglas. 2005. "Explaining the Rise in U.S. Antidumping Activity." *World Economy* 28(5): 651–668.

Johnson, Robert, and Guillermo Noguera. 2010. "Accounting for Intermediates: Production Sharing and Trade in Value Added." FREIT Working Paper No. 63. San Rafael, CA: Forum for Research in Empirical International Trade.

Koopman, Robert, William Powers, Zhi Wang, Shang-Jin Wei. 2010. "Give Credit Where Credit Is Due: Tracing Value Added in Global Production Chains." NBER Working Paper No. 16426. Cambridge, MA: National Bureau of Economic Research.

Koopman, Robert, Zhi Wang, and Shang-Jin Wei. 2008. "How Much Chinese Exports Is Really Made in China—Assessing Foreign and Domestic Value-Added in Gross Exports." NBER Working Paper 14109. Cambridge, MA: National Bureau of Economic Research.

———. 2010. "A World Factory in Global Production Chains: Estimating Imported Value-Added in Exports by the People's Republic of China." In *Costs and Benefits of Economic Integration in Asia*, Robert Barro and Jong-Wha Lee, eds. New York: Oxford University Press, pp. 241–253.

Krugman, Paul. 2008. "Trade and Wages, Reconsidered," Unpublished paper prepared for the Brookings Paper on Economic Activity. Princeton, NJ: Princeton University. http://www.princeton.edu/~pkrugman/pk-bpea-draft .pdf (accessed July 17, 2012).

———. 2010. "Chinese New Year." *New York Times*, January 1, A:29.

Lamy, Pascal. 2011. "Lamy Suggests 'Trade-In Value-Added' as a Better Measurement of World Trade." WTO News Item. http://www.wto.org/english/ news_e/news11_e/miwi_06jun11_e.htm (accessed October 3, 2012).

Lau, L.J., X. Chen, L.K. Cheng, K.C. Fung, Y. Sung, C. Yang, K. Zhu, J. Pei, and Z. Tang. 2007. "Non-Competitive Input-Output Model and Its Application: An Examination of the China-U.S. Trade Surplus." *Social Science in China* (5): 91–103 (in Chinese).

Rodrik, Dani. 2006. "What's So Special about China's Exports?" *China & World Economy* 14(5): 1–19.

Schott, Peter, 2008, "The Relative Sophistication of Chinese Exports." *Economic Policy* 53: 5–49.

Scott, Robert E. 2010. "Unfair China Trade Costs Local Jobs." Economic Policy Institute Briefing Paper No. 260. Washington, DC: Economic Policy Institute. http://www.epi.org/publications/entry/bp260/ (accessed July 17, 2012).

U.S. International Trade Commission (USITC). 2008. *Import Injury Investigations Case Statistics (FY 1980–2006)*. Report No. 01-08. http://www.usitc.gov/trade_remedy/USITC_Stat_Report-11-04-PUB.pdf (accessed July 17, 2012).

———. *The Economic Effects of Significant U.S. Import Restraints; Seventh Update; Special Topic: Global Supply Chains*. Investigation No. 332-325. Washington, DC: USITC. http://www.usitc.gov/publications/332/pub4253.pdf (accessed October 30, 2012).

Wang, Zhi, Marinos E. Tsigas, Jesse More, Xin Li, and Daniel Xu. 2010. "A Time Series Database for Global Trade, Production and Consumption Linkage." GTAP Resource No. 3391. West Lafayette, IN: Global Trade Analysis Project Resource. https://www.gtap.agecon.purdue.edu/resources/res_display.asp?RecordID=3391 (accessed July 17, 2012).

World Trade Organization and the Institute of Developing Economies–Japan External Trade Organization. 2011. *Trade Patterns and Global Value Chains in East Asia: From Trade in Goods to Trade in Tasks*. Washington, DC, and Mihama-Ku, Chiba, Japan: WTO and IDE-JETO.

Yao, Shunli. 2008. "Chinese Foreign Trade Performance and the China-U.S. Trade: 1995–2004—A Graphical Analysis Based on China Customs Statistics." USITC Office of Economics Working Paper No. 2008-03-A. Washington, DC: U.S. International Trade Commission.

Yi, Kei-Mu. 2003. "Can Vertical Specialization Explain the Growth of World Trade?" *Journal of Political Economy* 111(1): 52–102.

3

China's Economy from an American's Perspective

Gene H. Chang
University of Toledo

There have been many discussions about China's economy through-out the United States. Take an example from the Midwest. Years ago, the popular media focus was on cheap products made in China being sold in Walmart and Meijer, a regional grocery chain. Later, it was General Motors' joint venture and Kentucky Fried Chicken restaurants in China. Most recently, the focus has turned toward China's purchases of U.S. assets. It is no longer just about China investing in U.S. government bonds—in Toledo, Ohio, local news reports last year told of Mayor Michael Bell's sale of some city-owned properties to Chinese investors. After two trips to China, Bell succeeded in selling two water-front real estate properties for a total of $5 million, helping balance the city's budget. While the deal did cause some controversy, most people welcomed the injection of money into the city's strapped budget; in similar fashions across the country, people are realizing that China's economy has become very relevant not just on the national level, but also on the local level.

This chapter will focus on China's economy from an American's perspective by focusing on China's economic size, momentum, and potential, as well as the possible problems and hurdles China will face in the near future. Although there have been many discussions about China, there are also many misunderstandings too. As China is playing an increasingly important role in global affairs in the new century, the United States needs to be prepared to meet the challenges from China. A better understanding about China would help to improve policies of the bilateral relationship, so we can coexist in the new global economic order.

Perhaps the word that best describes China and its economy in the twenty-first century is *dynamic*. Here the word has multiple meanings: it means that the Chinese economy is expected to grow quickly and reshape the world economic map. It also means that China can impact the world economy in ways that the rest of the world may or may not appreciate. It also means that China has the potential to experience political or economic crises that could cause China's system to collapse and its economy to stagnate.

The West has complex views on China's increasing role in the world. In a 2011 global survey by the Pew Research Center on international opinions of whether China will overtake the United States as the largest economy, most Europeans think that China has already done so or soon will. Americans are equally divided between "yes" or "never" on this question. People in rival countries such as India and Japan are more doubtful. Yet, by any measure, there has been a significant change in the global attitude toward China compared to 10 years ago, when China's economic size was only a small fraction of that of the United States. To a large extent, the world is uncomfortable about a superpower that is under an authoritarian regime and ruled by a Communist Party. Among the same respondents, most (except for those in African and Muslim countries) consider China becoming the world's leading economic power as a bad thing.

In this chapter, I will discuss some seemingly straightforward subjects that often result in misunderstandings. They include the size of China's economy, trade with China, the kinds of challenges China poses to the United States, and China's own problems and weaknesses.

DIFFERENCES BETWEEN CHINA AND THE UNITED STATES

China and the United States are similar in physical size and climate zones, but in terms of topography, China is mostly mountainous and the United States is mostly flat. The resource endowments of both countries are similar, but China's population is more than four times that of the United States. The two countries are the largest economies in the world; however, in per capita terms, China is much poorer. In terms of social and economic development levels, China also significantly lags the United States. Table 3.1 lists the basic statistics of the two countries.

The economic relationship between the United States and China is crucially important for both countries because they depend on each other and they are integrated. The United States relies on China for cheap consumer products and for financing the U.S. debt, while China relies on the United States for export markets, technology, and foreign direct investment. China is the second-largest trade partner of the United States, with a total volume of imports and exports of $457 billion in 2010. Aside from multinational companies' intracompany, cross-border shipments between the United States and Canada, China is the United States' largest trading partner.

China's trade volume with the United States is 2.5 times the trade volume that the United States had with Japan (Table 3.2). U.S.-China trade is continuously expanding and shows no obvious signs of slowing down (Figure 3.1). In addition, China is the largest creditor of the United States, holding $1.12 trillion in U.S. Treasury bills, according to the U.S. Federal Reserve. However, scholars estimate that China actually holds an additional $700 billion in U.S. dollar denominated public

Table 3.1 China and the United States: Comparing Statistics and World Rankings

	China		United States	
	Statistics	World ranking	Statistics	World ranking
Population	1330 million	1	305 million	3
Area (sq. km.)	9.6 million	4	9.8 million	3
Climate	Diverse but mostly temperate		Diverse but mostly temperate	
Topography	Mostly mountainous		Mostly flat	
Renewable water	2,829 cu. km.	6	3,069 cu. km.	4
Economic size (GDP)	$6 trillion	3	$15 trillion	1
GDP per capita	4,382	94	$47,284	9
Life expectancy at birth (years)	73.5	105 (of 223 entities)	78.1	50 (of 223 entities)
Human development index	0.663	89 (out of 169)	0.902	4 (of 169)

Table 3.2 Top U.S. Trade Partners, 2010

	Country	Total trade volume ($, billions)
1	Canada	524.7
2	China	456.8
3	Mexico	393.0
4	Japan	180.9
5	Germany	130.9

SOURCE: http://www.census.gov/foreign-trade/top/dst/2010/12/balance.html (accessed June 26, 2012).

and private assets (such as Fannie Mae's bonds). These U.S. assets held by China are equivalent to 13 percent of the U.S. GDP. While the United States and China depend on each other, the two countries have frequent disagreements and disputes over a number of issues, such as trade, the environment, human rights, and military presence in the world.

Why has China become a top U.S. trading partner? The classical explanation is comparative advantage. China and the United States are very different in factor endowment: China has abundant cheap labor, with people willing to work for very low wages, while the United States has abundant capital and technology. China and the United States are complementary: China exports labor-intensive products, such as toys and textiles, to the United States, and the United States exports capital-intensive products, such as airplanes and generators, to China. The comparative advantage theory, however, does not fully explain the scale of trade. For instance, it cannot explain why Canada has a great scale of trade with the United States, as Canada has a similar factor endowment and thus is similar in comparative advantages to the United States. An alternative theory, called the gravity model, argues that trading volume is positively related with the country's economic size but negatively related with the spatial distance. Canada and Mexico are top trading partners of the United States because of the short geographical distance. China, Japan, and Western Europe are top trading partners because of their large economic sizes. In addition, unlike Canada, Japan, and Western Europe, China's industrial structure is more complementary with that of the United States, according to comparative advantages.

Figure 3.1 U.S. Trade and Trade Deficit with China, 1985–2011

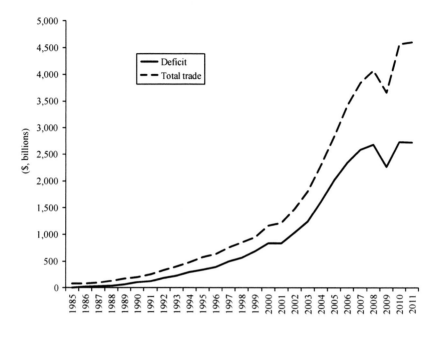

SOURCE: U.S. Census Bureau.

THE TRUE SIZE OF CHINA'S ECONOMY

How large is China's economy? The answer to this question has been a subject of some debate. Many scholars think that China's economy is actually larger than the number published by the Chinese government. As the Pew (2011) survey reveals, some people think that China has already overtaken the United States to become the world's largest economy. However, some scholars suggest that China's economy is smaller than the reported statistics. Admittedly, China's official statistics are not very reliable, as they can be influenced or even "cooked" for political reasons. Hence, let us first discuss the size of China's economy.

Using the official exchange rate and the figures reported by the State Statistics Bureau of China, China's GDP in 2010 was $5.7 trillion, ranking second in the world. This is about one-third of the United States'

**Figure 3.2 Size of China's Economy as Compared with the Largest
World Economies, 2010**

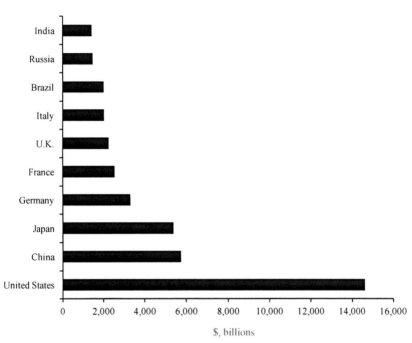

$, billions

SOURCE: World Bank, World Development Indicators, 2011.

GDP of $14.6 trillion. It is slightly larger than third-ranked Japan's GDP
of $5.4 trillion (Figure 3.2).

The regional gap between provinces in China is quite large, with
the coastal areas more developed than the inland. For instance, the
economy of Guangdong province, on the south coast, is equivalent to
the GDP of Indonesia, and the economies of Zhejiang and Jiangsu are
equivalent to those of Austria and Switzerland.

However, the official exchange rate often does not reflect the purchasing power of the currency. For instance, a Big Mac costs $3.73 in
the United States but costs 13.20 yuans in China, which converts to
only about $2.00 dollars. (The official exchange rate is 6.3 yuans to 1
dollar.) That means that the Chinese currency is probably undervalued
by the official exchange rate. The United Nations has conducted studies

Figure 3.3   China's Economy Measured by Purchasing Power Parity, 2010

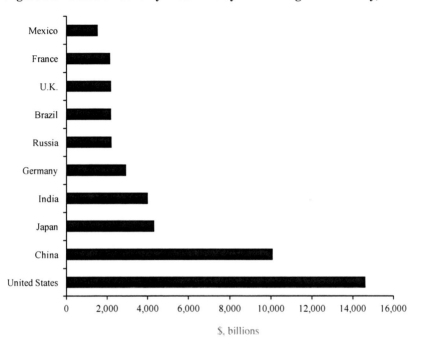

SOURCE: World Bank, World Development Indicators 2011, and http://www.wikipedia
.org (accessed June 2, 2011).

of the purchasing powers of different currencies, taking into account
their domestic prices. Converted by the purchasing power parity (PPP)
rate, the GDP of China in 2010 is $10.1 trillion, more than two-thirds
of that of the United States (Figure 3.3), and more than double that of
Japan.

On the other hand, Rawski (2001) argues that the Chinese economy
size is actually overstated and that the local cadres tend to exaggerate
the outputs for political gains. He uses the change in the number of airline passengers as a proxy for economic growth rate of China and sees
this number decline in 1997, yet the GDP reported by the government
grows by 7.8 percent. Therefore, he argues that China's growth rate
in 1997 may have only been 2–3 percent, or possibly even negative.
Rawski's argument is widely cited by the news media but refuted by
many scholars.

Most analysts, however, consider the Chinese data to be roughly correct, although few would deny that the official statistics are not independent of the Chinese government. The GDP figures in China are not systematically biased upward for a variety of reasons. First, local officials have more incentive to inflate the GDP growth rates rather than the absolute size because the GDP growth rate is a better indicator of the performance of their leadership. An overstated GDP size one year would adversely affect the growth rate figures for the following year. Secondly, the central government does not have an incentive to systematically overstate GDP figures. Sometimes it would even prefer a smaller growth rate in order to show that it is succeeding in controlling an overheating economy and containing inflation. To prevent the provinces from overstating the growth rates, the central government has some techniques to independently calculate and check the national growth rate using its own sampling survey teams from the state statistical bureau. As is often quoted in Western newspapers, the strange thing about Chinese statistics is that sometimes every province reports a higher growth rate than the national average. This is exactly due to inconsistencies between local and national figures when the central government does its own independent survey and publishes a smaller growth figure.

Rawski's (2001) argument was not supported by later updated GDP figures, either. Each year in January, the State Statistics Bureau publishes the preliminary GDP figure for the previous year. Later, when more updated and comprehensive data are available, the national figure is revised. The GDP figure is often revised upward, which actually refutes Rawski's argument. In 2006, the State Statistics Bureau lifted the GDP growth rate by an average of 0.5 percent a year between 1993 and 2004 to reflect the updated census results, which found that the economy in 2004 was 17 percent larger than previously reported. The only year for which the State Statistics Bureau did not revise GDP upward was 1998, when the bureau left it at 7.8 percent, a tacit admission that this figure at the time was exaggerated. One major reason for the 17 percent under-reported GDP was the missing value of some activities in the service sector. For instance, the business activities of restaurants, small stores, vendors, and barbers were often unreported or underreported. Many scholars, who point out that China's service sector is much smaller than other comparable countries, believe that even the current output of Chi-

Figure 3.4 Value Added by the Service Sector as Percentage of GDP in China, 2007

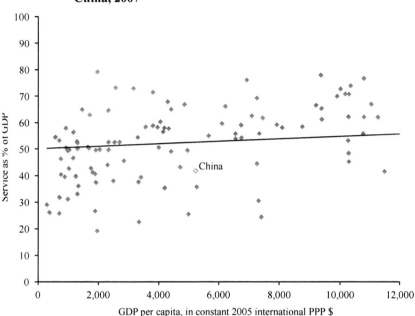

SOURCE: World Bank, World Development Indicators, 2011.

na's service sector remains undervalued. Figure 3.4 shows a regression result indicating that in 2007, China's service sector accounted for only 41 percent of GDP, which was 10 percent lower than the average for other countries at the same development level.

The GDP figure at PPP by the United Nations is probably a more reliable and comprehensive indicator of the true economic sizes of the nations in the world. Rawski's (2001) use of the number of airline passengers as a proxy of true GDP is not convincing, as airline travel is more a luxury good and thus not representative. If one has to use a commodity production as a proxy of GDP, economists often use the production of electricity. Electricity is used in production and consumption in almost every sector, so its production is a more representative indicator of the GDP size than the number of airline passengers. Figure 3.5 shows the electricity production by country in 2008. The United States ranks at the top by producing 4,140 billion kwh, and China ranks second at

Figure 3.5 Electricity Production by Country, 2008

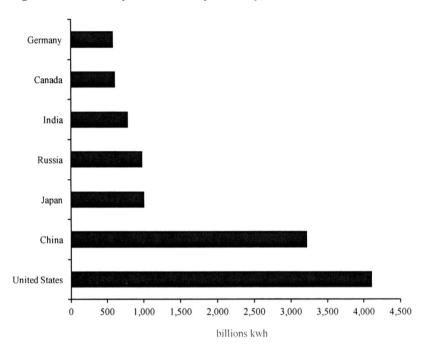

billions kwh

SOURCE: http://www.wikipedia.org (accessed June 6, 2011).

about two-thirds of the U.S. level. One can see that electricity production is roughly reflecting the GDP in PPP measures. In 2010, China's electricity production further grew to 4,140 billion kwh, matching the U.S. level in 2008. Hence, extrapolating from electricity production, Chinese GDP statistics seem generally consistent with its true size.

In terms of raw material and manufacturing industries, China is a dominant player in the world market. It has a great share of the world production in major raw materials, accounting for 50 percent of the global steel and cement production (Figure 3.6), which are mainly used for construction. Ten years ago, China produced about 2 million automobiles, much less than Japan, the United States, Germany, or South Korea. In 2010, China produced more than 18 million automobiles, roughly the sum of the total productions for both second-ranked Japan and third-ranked United States (Figure 3.7).

Figure 3.6 World Steel Production, 2009

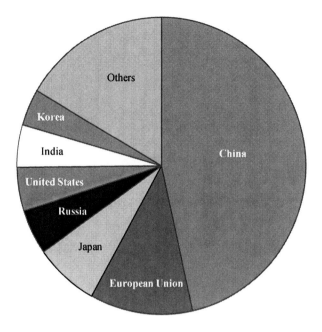

SOURCE: http://www.wikipedia.org (accessed June 1, 2011).

WHO WILL FEED CHINA?

Another controversial topic about China's economic capability is agricultural production. In 1995, Lester Brown wrote *Who Will Feed China?*, a book that spawned hundreds of conferences and seminars. He took a neo-Malthusian view about the prospects of the world food supply as China's income grows: "To feed its 1.2 billion people, China may soon have to import so much grain that this action could trigger unprecedented rises in world food (shortage) and prices" (p. 170). Now, nearly 20 years later, this scenario has not happened. China is still capable of feeding its population, although it imports corn and wheat, mostly as animal feed.

Figure 3.7 Automobile Production

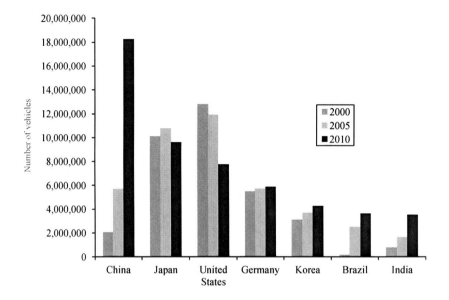

SOURCE: International Organization of Motor Vehicle Manufacturers, various years.

Let us look at the agriculture sector and compare the sector composition and production in China with other countries. Economic theory indicates that in the preindustrial period, agriculture contributes the most value added in a country's GDP. At the middle stage of industrialization, manufacturing and industry add the most value. At the developed stage, the service sector adds the most value in GDP. Table 3.3 illustrates the sector composition and production for China as compared with other countries. Its service sector is relatively small, adding value of $2.56 trillion, which is about 22 percent of that of the U.S. service sector. As previously mentioned, the value added in the service sector in China is undervalued because many small businesses were not reported. Supposing it is undervalued by 10 percent of GDP as predicted in the regression in Figure 3.4, China's service sector production would be $3.15 trillion, or 28 percent of that of the United States. In the industry sector, the value added is $2.75 trillion, which is 85 percent of the output of the U.S. industry. While agriculture in China accounts for less than 10 percent of GDP, it contributes a total of $564 billion, the

Table 3.3 Nominal GDP Sector Composition, 2010

Country	Nominal GDP	Agriculture %	Agriculture $, billions	Industry %	Industry $, billions	Services %	Services $, billions
United States	14,658	1.2	176	22.2	3,254	76.7	11,243
China	5,878	9.6	564	46.8	2,751	43.6	2,563
Japan	5,459	1.1	60	23.0	1,256	75.9	4,144
Germany	3,316	0.8	27	27.9	925	71.3	2,364
India	1,538	16.1	248	28.6	440	55.3	850

SOURCE: http://en.wikipedia.org/wiki/List_of_countries_by_GDP_sector_composition (accessed June 26, 2012).

largest in the world, and 320 percent of that of the United States. Yet, because of the large population size, China's agricultural output per capita ranks lower.

Most scholars dismissed Lester Brown's argument, although recently Brown has changed the tone to emphasize the need for a "wake-up call" about the deterioration of the global environment. During the past two decades, China's agriculture as well as its food supply continued to grow. Indeed, food production outpaced population growth in the past three decades (Figure 3.8). So far, the domestic supply and demand for food is basically balanced.

WILL CHINA OVERTAKE THE UNITED STATES AS THE LARGEST ECONOMY?

Since the beginning of the reform in 1978, China has experienced remarkable growth at an annual rate of around 10 percent for three decades, lifting hundreds of millions out of poverty. Figure 3.9 shows the average annual economic growth rate during the period of 1980–2009.

The global ranking of China's economy also moves upward quickly. In 2000, China's economy was still behind most large industrial economies. In the following years, China has passed the U.K., France, Germany, and Japan, one by one, and in 2010, it became the second-largest economy (Figure 3.10). While it is still smaller than the United States in terms of GDP, because of China's faster growth, China now contributes

Figure 3.8 Food Production Outpaces Population Growth in China (2000 = 100)

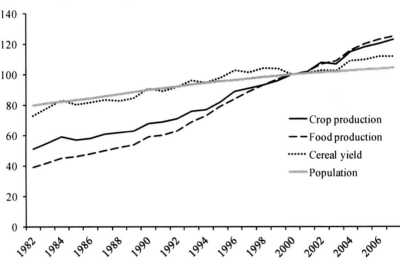

SOURCE: World Bank, World Development Indicators, 2009.

more to global growth than the United States. Multiplying the GDP size by the growth rate, in 2010 China contributed $574 billion while the United States contributed $393 billion.

If this trend continues, China will overtake the United States to become the largest economy by 2020 (Figure 3.11). We can attribute this rapid change in China's ranking to two previous events, but we have to assume that they continue in the next 10 years: 1) economic growth continues at around 9–10 percent, and 2) China's currency appreciates as income increases, due to both the elimination of the existing misalignment of the undervalued Chinese currency renminbi (RMB) and the diminishing Balassa-Samuelson effect. Taking into account the factors for currency appreciation, RMB has the potential to appreciate 5 percent each year for another 10 years. Measuring China's GDP by PPP rather than the market exchange rate would also contribute to this change in ranking. When China's economy grows, the price level will gradually approach that of the developed countries; in other words, the difference between nominal GDP and PPP GDP would diminish. China's GDP by PPP is about two-thirds of the U.S. GDP right now.

Figure 3.9 Average Annual GDP Growth Rate, 1980–2009

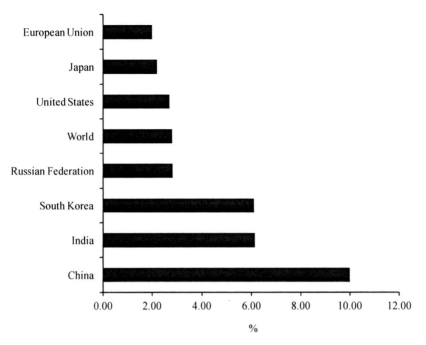

SOURCE: World Bank, World Development Indicators, 2010.

Assuming the U.S. economy grows at a rate of 3–4 percent, and China grows at 10 percent, one can calculate that China's PPP GDP would catch that of the United States by the end of this decade. Of course, if China's growth slows down in the coming years, it would take a longer time to catch up with the United States.

What explains the rapid and sustained economic growth of China for three decades? Reasons range from Chinese culture to purely timing, and none are uncontroversial. Below, I will focus on some obvious economic reasons, namely, the high rate of capital formation (investment in fixed capital), supported by the high rate of saving. In terms of fixed capital investment and saving as percentages of GDP, China is ranked near the top of the world (Figure 3.12).

China spends 45.6 percent of its GDP on fixed capital formation (Figure 3.12). The country is enthusiastic in spending on infrastructure, residential housing, and equipment, and it is never timid about pouring

Figure 3.10 GDP by Country, 1998–2010

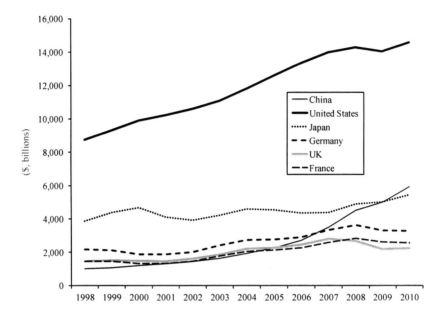

SOURCE: World Development Indicators, 2009, 2011.

money into huge projects, which is partially due to the authoritarian regime that does not need taxpayers to approve the spending. Local governments are even more zealous about spending because large projects are symbols of their performance; they get credits for building big projects in their local areas, but they are not actually held accountable for the cost. The investment funds often come from loans by local state-owned banks. If the loans finally go bad, it is hard to determine exactly who was responsible for the bad decision. Ultimately, the state picks up the tab. Kornai (1980) calls this behavior under such a system the "soft budget constraint." The true scales of construction and other investment projects are even larger than the reported figures in the official statistics, as the local officials tend to underreport their investment to avoid the discipline from the central government's macroeconomic contractionary measures. As a result, construction is everywhere in China. A common impression of a foreign visitor to China is that the entire country

Figure 3.11 Projections for GDP

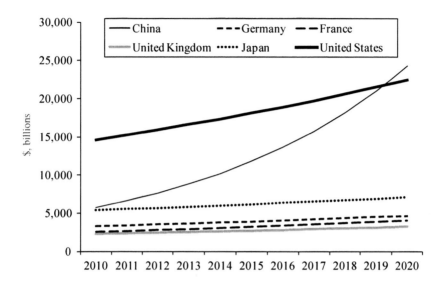

SOURCE: Author's calculations.

looks like a construction site, and construction cranes become the symbol of the national bird.

Ironically, the zealous drive for investment helps the Chinese economy in special situations. In the economic recession following the financial crisis of 2008, the love for investment helped the economy to recover. In 2008, when the financial crisis spread to China, exports and production dropped, and many factories closed. In Guangdong and its neighboring provinces, more than 20 million workers lost their jobs. In December 2008, China's Politburo convened a meeting, and within two days, the country announced a US$600 billion equivalent stimulus package for the following two years. The package included a nationwide high-speed rail system project with a 10-year plan of $300 billion, and 50 nuclear power projects (one-third of the global total planned) in addition to the 27 already under construction. Then, the stimulus package of the central government was further amplified by the local governments. One calculation is that the local governments' spending plans together added another $2.4 trillion. It was also implemented quickly;

Figure 3.12 Fixed Capital Investment and Saving as Percentage of GDP, 2009

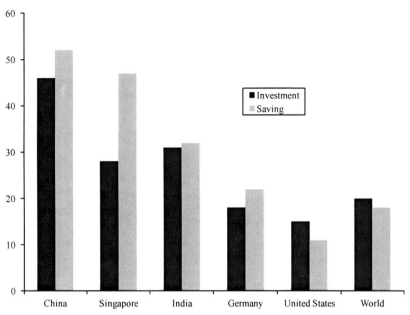

NOTE: Data for Singapore are from 2008.
SOURCE: World Bank, World Development Indicators, 2010.

several days after the announcement and before the beginning of 2009, the money started to distribute through the nationwide banks. Despite the waste and corruption that was involved in the process, the stimulus worked. Most of the laid-off workers from closed factories in Guangdong found jobs in railroad construction or other projects. The private sector also followed the government's lead, particularly by expanding residential housing construction and providing supplies to the state-sponsored projects (Figure 3.13). Within several months, the economy started to recover as the Keynesian multiplier predicts. The economy turned around and growth reached 8.7 percent in 2009. By 2010, the economy was fully recovered from recession, and inflation became the main threat instead.

In contrast, the U.S. government had difficulties reaching an agreement on spending. Many believed the U.S. stimulus package was too

Figure 3.13 New Residential Building Construction, 2010

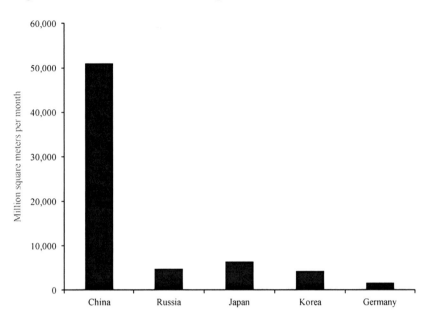

SOURCE: United Nations.

little, too conservative, and too late. Since the stimulus was announced, there has been little money spent on new infrastructure projects or other fixed capital investments. Thus, the economic recession continues and high unemployment remains even today.

The money for capital investment comes from public and private saving in China, which accounts for more than half (52 percent) of the GDP (Figure 3.12). For each yuan the Chinese made, they spent less than half in consumption. Why is the savings rate so high in China? Most scholars would give the following list of explanations, in line with conventional theories:

- Rapid growth in income. As personal income rises rapidly, old habits remain, hence consumption increase lags behind income increase.

- A relatively younger population composition, so the larger working population provides a "demographic dividend."

• The influence of the Confucian culture and thrifty habits by the older generations.

• A lack of social security and high cost of education for the children, so households have to save a lot to take precaution.

There are also some unconventional arguments for the high saving in China. Wei and Zhang (2011) argue that it was due to the one-child policy and preference for boys. As a result, illegal abortion of female fetuses still happens often in rural China, causing a shortage of girls. This leads to a competitive marriage market and rapidly rising marriage costs. Parents must save a lot in order to purchase an apartment for their sons, as it has become a prerequisite for marriage (apartments are very expensive in China and typically cost US$500,000 in large cities for a three-bedroom unit).

TRADE AND THE CHINESE CURRENCY ISSUE

Among all the U.S.-China relationship issues, the trade deficit with China has produced the most media headlines. China has been the largest trade deficit source for the United States for years. In 2010, the United States had a trade deficit of $273 billion with China—the largest ever recorded. The trade deficit with China is even larger than the deficits the United States has with the next four ranked countries (Mexico, Japan, Germany, and Canada) combined (Table 3.4). Further, the trend of the growing total trade volume and trade deficit with China is continuing and does not seem likely to reverse in the near future (see Figure 3.1.)

It should be noted that China's trade deficit with the United States is a special case, as China runs much fewer trade surpluses with other countries. China's global trade surplus in 2010 is $183 billion, which means that once the surplus with the United States is excluded, China is running an aggregate deficit with other countries. In the first quarter of 2011, China even ran a global trade deficit. In 2010, China overtook Germany as the world's largest exporter, but it is still a greater importer than Germany (China is the second-largest importer behind the United States). Hence, the global trade surplus of China is smaller than Germany ($183 billion versus $204 billion in 2010).

Table 3.4 Top Countries with which the U.S. Has a Trade Deficit, 2010 ($, billions)

1	China	273.0
2	Mexico	66.4
3	Japan	59.8
4	Germany	34.5
5	Canada	28.2

SOURCE: U.S. Census Bureau. http://www.census.gov/foreign-trade/top/dst/2010/12/balance.html (accessed January 3, 2011).

U.S. politicians and news media often blame undervalued currency for the deficit with China, though most economists would consider a lower gross saving amount as a more important factor for the U.S. trade deficit. Germany has an overvalued euro, but it is running a trade surplus with the United States and even a large trade surplus with China. The Canadian dollar is overvalued against the U.S. dollar, but it ran a trade surplus with the United States in 2010.

From my calculation (Chang 2011), China's currency is indeed undervalued. The Chinese currency is 25 percent undervalued against the U.S. dollar, but 17 percent undervalued against the global balance equilibrium value because the U.S. dollar is about 10 percent overvalued against its global balance equilibrium value. China's trade surplus with the United States is particularly large, partly because unlike the Euro zone and Japan, China keeps the RMB relatively stable with the U.S. dollar, thus reducing the foreign exchange cost in trade between China and the United States. Hence, American importers particularly prefer to trade with China due to lower and predictable transaction costs. Another reason is that China has become the major processing zone for the U.S. market with the help of many Taiwanese, Japanese, and U.S. companies. These companies import inputs from other countries, process in China, and finally export to the United States. This largely explains why China runs an overall trade deficit with other countries but runs a huge trade surplus with the United States.

China also has an overwhelming presence in the international monetary market due to its huge foreign exchange reserves and its possession of an increasing amount of U.S. debt. China had $3.1 trillion in foreign reserves as of June 2011. According to the Fed's records, China owns about $1.12 trillion of U.S. government securities. In addition,

China owns other American dollar assets worth about $800 billion. The main reason for the recent swelling foreign exchange reserve in China is not because of the current account surplus, but because of a large amount of international floating capital flowing into China, speculating on the rise of yuan, and looking for better returns in emerging economies. The huge foreign reserve is not a blessing but rather a curse for China as it increases the inflationary pressure. Hence, China is now accelerating the appreciation of yuan, and at the same time, encouraging its citizens to travel and invest overseas, to reduce the oversupply of the foreign reserves.

CHINA'S CHALLENGES

China is poised to be a rising power to the United States and the world in this twenty-first century, yet China itself faces challenges in the future. China has potential to be a great power, but also the potential to fail and implode. The Communist political authoritarian system, in particular, is unstable. When the Communist authoritarian system collapses, the resulting political and economic crisis could dwarf an economic recession.

China is a huge economy, but with a population of 1.3 billion people, China is still poor; the GDP per capita is low, ranking 94th in the world. Figure 3.14 shows the comparison between China and the United States in major indicators that relate to a country's status and potential. In the figure, China's numbers are measured as the percentages of those of the United States. The indicators include GDP per capita, renewable water per capita, energy consumption per capita, Environmental Sustainable Index (ESI index), and fertility. China lags substantially behind the United States in these measures. Given the limited resources per capita that China possesses, if China continues the current production pattern at the current growth rate, its resources will be depleted at an unsustainable rate. Unless China can successfully transform its current growth pattern, China would hit a resource bottleneck in the near future.

China's fertility dropped to 1.54 in 2010, and the population will age quickly in the coming years. This sets up a "demographic time bomb" for the future. By the year 2050, the dependent ratio would reach

Figure 3.14 China's Weakness: China Compared with the United States, 2010 (U.S. = 100)

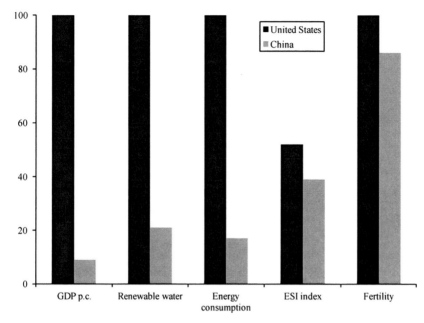

SOURCE: World Bank, United Nations, 2011.

80 percent, and the elderly would make up more than 30 percent of the population. Figure 3.15 shows the projected demographics.

To change its growth pattern from the current labor-intensive economy to one that is more technology intensive, China needs to increase highly skilled human capital. Yet, the current educational system and limits on technology do not promote creative thinking, research, and development, which are crucial for growth. At a time when information is a key to economic success, the information flow in China is often censored under the current Communist political system. The Internet censorship by the filter "Great Wall" often blocks necessary information, from soft science to hard science—an unintended consequence that impedes economic growth. Scholars and scientists cannot access information or references that are necessary for research. In addition, China's education system is corrupted. Under the current system, rewards and research grants are often allocated based on who has politi-

Figure 3.15 China's Demographic Time Bomb

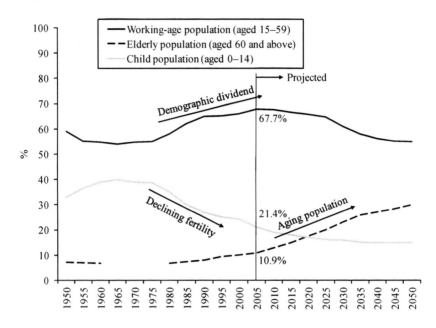

SOURCE: Reprinted with permission from Kwan (2006).

cal influence or personal connections rather than on merit. As a result, professors and researchers focus on short-term quick gains rather than long-term investment and research projects. There is no serious and effective legal system to protect intellectual property rights; hence, truly original innovation is discouraged. Currently China's technology is much behind that of the United States, but with such an ineffective or corrupted system as described above, the gap does not seem likely to close in advanced areas in the near future.

Corruption and inefficiency are rampant in China. Journalist Garnaut describes "corruption in China growing at least as fast as the economy" (Garnaut 2010). Recently, a government audit report showed that embezzlers stole 187 million yuan, or roughly $28.5 million, from the Beijing-to-Shanghai portion of the high-speed railway project, resulting in the arrest of Railway Minister Liu Zhijun and his associate Zhang Shuguang (*Beijing Morning Newspaper* 2011).

Table 3.5 Income Gap in China

Country	Gini coefficient
Sweden	0.230
Taiwan	0.330
United Kingdom	0.340
U.S.	0.450
China	0.469
Brazil	0.567

SOURCE: Wikipedia.org, originally from U.N. Gini data, 2011.

China's income gap is widening, frequently causing social and political conflict and unrest. The Gini index reaches 0.469 for China, which is higher than most countries in the world (Table 3.5). The Chinese Communist government lacks the legitimacy to rule because it is not elected by people, and lacks much confidence from the common people. There is no independent legal system or channel where people can vent their grievances or trust they will be treated objectively. Hence, there exists a widespread hatred toward the governments and their officials, causing unrest and protests—there were 220,000 recorded incidents of protest in 2009. Under the current system, China is politically unstable, and a large-scale protest that topples the government is possible in the future.

Under the Chinese Communist authoritarian system, China lacks rule of law. The party determines everything, hence impeding not only creativity and independent thinking but also entrepreneurship. Furthermore, private property is still not protected. An increasing number of leftist Maoists are now calling for a revolution to expropriate the properties of the newly rich. Hu Jintao has done little to stop the Maoist leftists, which alarms many private entrepreneurs. As a result, there is an increasing number of rich or just well-to-do Chinese seeking emigration to the West, and billions of dollars of capital are flying from China to the United States and other immigration destinations such as Canada and Australia.

Reformists in the party are concerned about the potentially dangerous situation. In his recent overseas trips, Premier Wen Jiabao called for political and economic reforms. On the table, he said, is government transparency, creating an environment where people and the media can criticize and supervise the government. However, it is widely reported that Wen represents only the minority in the party and that the conservatives opposing political reform are dominant.

CONCLUSION

China is a dynamic country, and one should never be surprised when significant events occur there, good or bad. China is a large economy with a great momentum, but it is still a poor country in per capita terms and has many domestic problems. China is dynamic with surprises and uncertainties. Do not be surprised if in the near future China overtakes the United States in GDP, makes the most airplanes in the world, or suffers the fallout of a political uprising that breaks down the system. In the interest of China, the United States, and the rest of the world, we hope China can gradually move forward to economic prosperity and political democracy.

References

Beijing Morning Newspaper. 2011. March 24, http://news.sina.com.cn/c/2011 -03-24/011522169359.shtml (accessed June 26, 2012).

Brown, Lester. 1995. *Who Will Feed China?* Worldwatch Institute, Environmental Alert Series. New York: W.W. Norton & Company.

Chang, Gene H. 2011. "Theory and Refinement of the Enhanced-PPP Model for Equilibrium Exchange Rates." Photocopy. Toledo, OH: University of Toledo.

Garnaut, John. 2010. "Corruption in China Growing at Least as Fast as the Economy." *The Age.* http://www.theage.com.au/world/corruption-in-china -growing-at-least-as-fast-as-the-economy-20100108-lyxe.html   (accessed June 26, 2012).

Kornai, Janos. 1980. *Economics of Shortage.* Amsterdam: North Holland Publisher.

Kwan, C.H. 2006. "China Facing the Challenge of Aging Population." Research Institute of Economy, Trade and Industry, IAA, Tokyo. http://www.rieti .go.jp/en/china/06112801.html (accessed July 18, 2012).

Pew Research Center. 2011. *U.S. Favorability Ratings Remain Positive: China Seen Overtaking U.S. as Global Superpower: 23-Nation Pew Global Atti-*

tudes Survey. Washington, DC: Pew Research Center. http://pewglobal
.org/2011/07/13/china-seen-overtaking-us-as-global-superpower/ (accessed
January 3, 2011).

Rawski, Thomas. 2001. "What Is Happening to China's GDP Statistics?" *China Economic Review* 12(4): 347–354.

Wei, Shang-jin, and Xiaobo Zhang. 2011. "The Competitive Saving Motive: Evidence from Rising Sex Ratios and Savings Rates in China." *Journal of Political Economy* 119(3): 511–564.

4
Winners and Losers in China's Economic Reform

Terry Sicular
University of Western Ontario

More than three decades have passed since China began to transform its economy. With this economic transformation has come rapid growth in both national income (GDP) and household incomes. Widening inequality has also emerged. China's increasing income inequality has been documented in numerous studies, including Benjamin et al. (2008); Ravallion and Chen (2007); Gustafsson, Li, and Sicular (2008); Wan (2008); and World Bank (2009).

This chapter discusses recent trends in inequality in China, with a focus on the period from 2002 onward, during which time China's government adjusted its economic development strategy to underscore balanced growth. Prior to 2002, under the leadership of Jiang Zemin, China's policies emphasized rapid growth. Growth was indeed rapid, but by the end of the Jiang era concerns had emerged about sustainability, both politically and environmentally. After Hu Jintao and Wen Jiabao assumed leadership in 2002–2003, a new development strategy was announced that emphasized sustainable and harmonious growth. The new strategy, referred to as the "Scientific Vision of Development," placed emphasis on balanced development and implemented a series of policies to reduce disparities and protect the economically vulnerable. Measures adopted included agricultural support policies, social welfare transfers, targeted tax reductions, minimum wage increases, and increased spending on poverty alleviation.

What happened after the adoption of the new strategy? After 2002 China's economy continued to grow rapidly; indeed, the size of the GDP pie roughly doubled by the late 2000s. But what happened to the distribution of that pie? Did inequality continue to rise, or was it moderated? What happened to poverty levels?

Economists have long thought that economic development is initially accompanied by rising inequality, but that eventually forces emerge that will cause inequality to decline. This "inverted U" relationship between growth and inequality is called the Kuznets hypothesis, first proposed by Simon Kuznets (1955). The logic is that initially growth begins in certain sectors and regions, and the benefits of early growth therefore go to a small subset of the population, causing inequality to increase. As development continues, however, under the right conditions, growth will spread to other sectors and regions. Employment will expand, and the benefits of growth will be shared more widely. In the long term, inequality can decline. Rising inequality is therefore not necessarily a permanent feature of growth in general or in China.

In this chapter I review findings of past studies and present new evidence on trends in inequality and poverty in China for the period 2002–2007. The new evidence is based on joint research with Li Shi and Luo Chuliang (Beijing Normal University), and Yue Ximing (Renmin University of China) using nationwide household survey data collected under the China Household Income Project (CHIP). It constitutes the first systematic evidence on inequality and poverty in China during the Hu-Wen era.

Overall, we find that as of 2007 China had not yet reached the Kuznets turning point. The benefits of growth between 2002 and 2007 were not shared equally: richer urban groups benefited more than poorer, rural groups. Nevertheless, both the poor and the rich saw their incomes grow, and poverty declined. Thus, some groups have "won" more than others, but we do not find evidence of many losers.

DATA AND MEASUREMENT

The data used in our analysis come from the four waves of household surveys conducted by CHIP, which collected data for 1988, 1995, 2002, and 2007. These surveys cover urban households (mainly formal urban residents with local urban registration, or *hukou*) and rural households. The samples of urban households and rural households are subsamples of the larger urban and rural household income surveys conducted by the National Bureau of Statistics (NBS). In 2002 and 2007 independent samples of rural-to-urban migrants were added. When combined with weights, the surveys are nationally representative, but migrants are underrepresented in earlier years of the CHIP survey. However, migration was fairly modest before the late 1990s, so the resulting bias is likely not substantial.

We measure income in per capita terms (household income divided by the number of household members). Income here is disposable (after tax) income, which includes wage earnings; pension income; net income from farming and self-employment; income from assets; in-kind and self-produced income; and transfers and subsidies, minus taxes. Asset income includes imputed rental income on owner-occupied housing. Imputed rent is the implicit earning on investment in housing, parallel to the returns to other assets such as interest earnings on savings deposits. We follow the literature and calculate imputed rental income on owner-occupied housing as a rate of return on the market value of owned housing.

INEQUALITY

Our measure of inequality is the Gini coefficient, a commonly used index of inequality that takes a value between 0 and 1. A Gini of 0 would mean perfect equality—all members of the society have identical, equal income. A Gini of 1 would indicate perfect inequality—one person has all of the society's income, and everyone else has no income. No real society has perfect equality or perfect inequality. The Gini coefficients for actual countries mostly range from 0.20 (very low inequality) to 0.70 (very high inequality).

Figure 4.1 shows income inequality in China measured in each of the four years of the CHIP survey. For comparability across years, inequality is measured without including migrants (including migrants in 2002 and 2007 in fact changes national inequality only slightly).

As reported widely in many studies, inequality rose substantially between the 1980s and mid-1990s. Factors contributing to rising inequality at this time included growing regional and provincial income

Figure 4.1 Income Inequality in China, 1988–2007

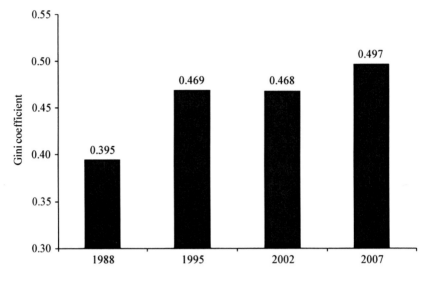

SOURCE: CHIP.

differences, a widening gap between urban and rural incomes, income disparities associated with educational differences, and in rural areas unequal access to higher-paying off-farm employment.

Between 1995 and 2002, inequality in China remained roughly constant, suggesting that perhaps China had reached the Kuznets turning point. Gustafsson, Li, and Sicular (2008) provide a detailed analysis of inequality in these years and identify the emergence of some inequality-reducing factors. Some regions and provinces that had lagged behind others in the first period began to catch up. Rural off-farm employment became more widespread, contributing to a decline in rural inequality. Macroeconomic growth during this period was widely shared. Nevertheless, other disequalizing factors—the urban-rural gap and education-based income disparities—continued.

From 2002 to 2007 inequality resumed its upward trend. China had not yet reached the Kuznets turning point. By 2007, in fact, inequality in China had reached a level that was quite high by international standards. Figure 4.2 shows Gini coefficients for a selection of countries. In 2007 China's Gini coefficient of 0.497 approached those of what are considered to be high inequality countries such as Mexico and Zambia, although it was still lower than the extremely high Gini coefficients found in countries like Brazil and Colombia.

Several factors appear to have contributed to the upward trend in inequality between 2002 and 2007. Within rural and urban areas, levels of inequality did not increase substantially; however, the gap between urban and rural incomes continued to widen. In 2007 urban incomes per capita on average were 4.1 times rural incomes. This ratio was up from 3.3 in 2002, which was already high by international standards. In other countries for which data are available, the ratio of urban to rural incomes ranges from below 2 in countries like India, Indonesia, and Malaysia to 2.2–2.3 in the Philippines and Thailand, to over 3 in countries like Zambia and South Africa. China is at or near the top of this range.

We have used inequality decomposition by group to calculate the contribution of the urban-rural income gap to overall inequality. We

Figure 4.2 Inequality: Country Comparisons

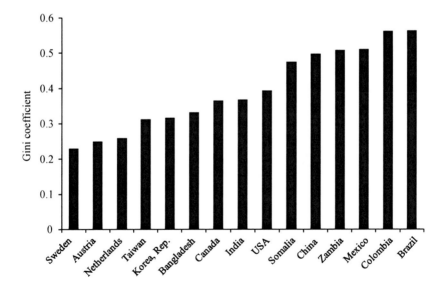

NOTE: Years are all 2005 or earlier, except for China, which is 2007.
SOURCE: UNU-WIDER (2008) and CHIP.

find that in 2002 the urban-rural income gap contributed an already large 46–47 percent of overall inequality in China. In 2007 the contribution had risen to 51–54 percent.

A second factor contributing to inequality has been household income from assets and property. During the Maoist era most property was nationalized or collectivized, and households owned little private property. In the 1990s major property rights reforms were implemented that gave households opportunities to own property. These reforms included the privatization of urban housing, the development of the urban real estate market, enterprise ownership reforms, and the expansion of stock and financial markets.

In the wake of these and other measures, household income from assets and property, including imputed rents from owner-occupied housing, rose to 10 percent of household income in 2002, and further to 15 percent in 2007. Asset income in China is unequally distributed, and its contribution to inequality has increased. A decomposition of income by source reveals that the contribution of income from assets and property to national inequality increased from 9 percent in 2002 to 20 percent in 2007.

The rise in inequality between 2002 and 2007 implies that some households benefited more and others less from growth during this period. Who, then, were the winners and losers? Figure 4.3 shows growth in household income by decile groups in the population. Each bar shows the level of income in 2007, measured in constant 2002 dollars. The bottom portion of the bar is the level of income in 2002, and the top portion of the bar is the change in income between 2002 and 2007, expressed in constant 2002 dollars.

All decile groups, from the poorest 10 percent of the population at the far left to the richest 10 percent at the far right, enjoyed positive growth in income between the two years. Growth in income of the poorest decile, however, was much smaller in both percentage and absolute terms than that of the richest decile. Income of the poorest decile increased by 406 yuan, less than 50 percent of 2002 income. Income of the richest decile increased by nearly 16,000 yuan, or roughly doubled. For intermediate deciles, growth in income was correlated closely to their position in the income distribution.

Figure 4.3 thus shows that all income groups were "winners" during this period. Yet, some groups benefited more than others. This pattern

Figure 4.3 Per Capita Household Income by Decile, 2002 and 2007

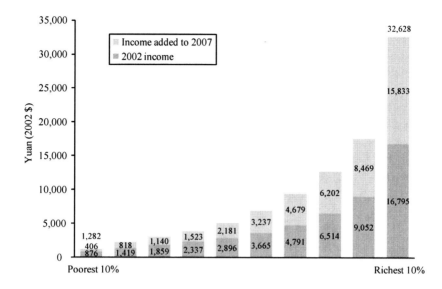

SOURCE: CHIP.

of income growth across deciles is of course associated with the rising inequality we have found during this period.

POVERTY: WHAT HAPPENED TO THE MOST VULNERABLE?

Changes in poverty levels are an important indicator of the impact of growth on the distribution of income. Regardless of whether the gap between poor and rich individuals increases, we care whether welfare improved for the poorest and most vulnerable members of society.

Poverty can be measured in different ways. Here I present estimates of the poverty head count—the number of people below a poverty line—and the poverty rate—the share of the population below the poverty line. Studies of poverty in China have used a range of poverty lines. The World Bank's standard poverty line of $1.25 a day (measured in purchasing power parity prices) is widely used for China and also for other countries, and we use it in our analysis. Other poverty lines typically yield similar trends in poverty levels over time.

Figure 4.4 shows estimates of poverty through 2002 from Chen and Ravallion (2008). Both the number of poor and the poverty rate declined dramatically between the early 1990s and early 2000s. Whereas in 1993 the poverty rate was 40 percent, by 2002 it had fallen to 15 percent. This dramatic decline in poverty was in part due to economic growth, which raised many poor above the poverty line, and in part due to a range of policies aimed at lagging regions and poverty alleviation.

Analysis of poverty using the CHIP data for 2002 and 2007 reveals that China's poverty levels continued to decline during the Hu-Wen period. The CHIP data give slightly lower poverty rates in 2002 than

Figure 4.4 Poverty in China 1993–2002, at $1.25/day

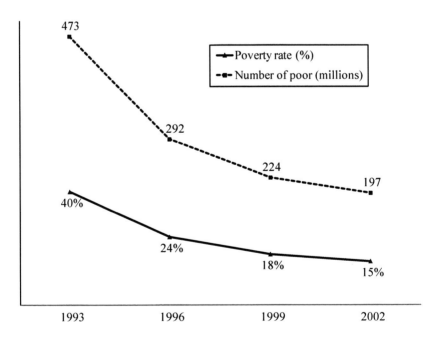

SOURCE: Chen and Ravallion (2008).

reported in the Chen and Ravallion (2008) study, but here we are mainly interested in the trend or change over time. As shown in Figure 4.5, based on the CHIP data, the poverty rate declined further between 2002 and 2007, from 10 percent to less than 4 percent. Most of this decline is due to a steep reduction in rural poverty.

China's success in reducing poverty is outstanding by international standards. As a consequence of these trends, China has changed from a high-poverty country to a moderately low-poverty country (Figure 4.6). Moreover, China's share of world poverty has declined substantially, from nearly 40 percent of the world's poor in 1990 to only 15 percent in 2005 (World Bank 2009).

Figure 4.5 Poverty in China (%), 2002–2007, at \$1.25/day

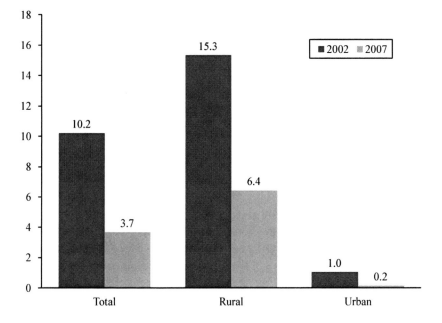

SOURCE: CHIP.

Figure 4.6 Poverty Rates: Country Comparisons, 2005–2006 ($1.25/day)

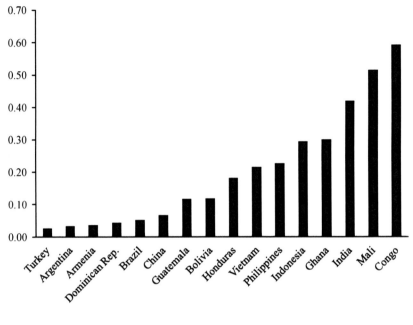

SOURCE: CHIP.

CONCLUSIONS

Despite official rhetoric during the Hu-Wen period emphasizing shared growth, inequality in China continued to rise during their tenure, at least through 2007. Factors contributing to the expansion of inequality include further widening of the already large urban-rural income gap and the emergence of private property, which is distributed unequally. Inequality in income from property and assets is potentially a hot button issue, as China's urban housing reform was not transparent or equitable, and more generally due to ongoing rent seeking in real estate and enterprise ownership.

China has achieved major progress in poverty reduction. Nevertheless, although fewer people are poor in absolute terms, that is, relative to an absolute poverty line, relative poverty may be on the rise. If we measure poverty in relative terms as the share of the population with incomes below 50 percent of median income, then we find that poverty increased from 12 percent in 2002 to 15 percent in 2007. While this increase in relative poverty is modest, it indicates that households at the bottom of the income distribution are falling further behind relative to those in the middle and top of the distribution. As China's economy matures and the number of absolute poor shrinks, relative poverty will become an increasingly important social indicator.

In summary, we find that China's economic reforms have had many winners and few absolute losers. Yet, challenges to China's harmonious society are ongoing. With development, the target has shifted, and China's policies will need to evolve accordingly.

References

Benjamin, Dwayne, Loren Brandt, John Giles, and Wang Sangui. 2008. "Income Inequality during China's Economic Transition." In *China's Great Economic Transition*, Loren Brandt and Thomas G. Rawski, eds. New York: Cambridge University Press, pp. 729–775.

Chen, Shaohua, and Martin Ravallion. 2008. "China Is Poorer Than We Thought, but Still No Less Successful in the Fight against Poverty." World Bank Research Working Paper No. WPS4621. Washington, DC: World Bank.

Gustafsson, Björn, Li Shi, and Terry Sicular, eds. 2008. *Inequality and Public Policy in China.* New York: Cambridge University Press.

Kuznets, Simon. 1955. "Economic Growth and Income Inequality." *American Economic Review* 45(1): 1–28.

Ravallion, Martin, and Chen Shaohua. 2007. "China's (Uneven) Progress against Poverty." *Journal of Development Economics* 82: 1–42.

UNU-WIDER, World Inequality Database. 2008. Version 2.0c. http://www.wider.unu.edu/research/Database/en_GB/database/ (accessed October 2010).

Wan, Guanghua, ed. 2008. *Inequality and Growth in Modern China.* New York: Oxford University Press.

World Bank. 2009. *From Poor Areas to Poor People: China's Evolving Poverty Reduction Agenda—An Assessment of Poverty and Inequality in China.* Washington, DC: World Bank, Poverty Reduction and Economic Management Department, East Asia and Pacific Region.

5

Changes in the World's Workshop

The Demographic, Social, and Political Factors behind China's Labor Movement

Mary Gallagher
University of Michigan

Labor strikes in southern China in the spring of 2010 awakened China watchers around the world to the possibility of a new wave of labor activism in China. The People's Republic of China has experienced labor strife before. During the reform period alone, the state has had to deal with autonomous worker organizations during the 1989 student movement; a large but regionally bounded spate of protests against the state sector restructuring at the turn of the century; and, since 1995, a steady, inexorable rise in the number of individual workers who sue their employers each year. In most analyses, however, the Chinese state is portrayed as adept in reining in challenges to the labor status quo. A truism is to state that there has yet to be a major labor movement that spans regional and workplace divisions. Workers may be angry but they are angry alone, not collectively.

In this chapter, I introduce the general state of labor conditions in China while highlighting three important contextual changes that have occurred in the last decade. These contextual changes are important in understanding the current developments in labor activism and future potential for greater social instability around the issues of workplace rights and conditions and employment. The shifts in the demographic, social, and political context of workers in China have put pressure on the development model adopted by the Chinese state since the early 1990s, which relies on cheap labor and labor-intensive manufacturing as key factors in rapid growth. As the foundations for this model diminish, local governments in China are pressured to find new sources of economic dynamism. If successful, China's transition away from this development model to a more sustainable, consumer-driven economy will herald China's arrival on the world stage as the key rising challenger to the United States. There are, however, many roadblocks on the path to middle- and high-income country status, especially for a country as large and regionally diverse as China. Labor issues are a key source of social instability and have been highlighted by high levels in the leadership as a focal point for policy reform and "stability preservation" policies.

CHINA'S CHANGING DEMOGRAPHIC CONTEXT

In the 1990s, it was a surety among economists and foreign investors that China's rural labor supply was virtually unlimited. Tens of millions of migrant workers poured into coastal developmental areas each year looking for the first factory jobs and opportunities to earn money, gain experience, and better the life chances of their kids, if not themselves. In 2003, to the surprise of many, there were reports in the Chinese media of a "migrant labor shortage" (民工荒) in development zones in China's south. Although this shortage ebbed during the global financial crisis and China's export crisis of 2008–2009, these shortages began to reappear soon after. Economists also noted that migrant wages, after a long period of relative stagnation, were growing quickly.

As Yang (2011a), Cai (2008), and Cai and Wang (2011) have noted, China's demographic changes since the 1980s have been particularly beneficial in fueling rapid export growth and industrialization. This "double demographic dividend" is the result of two different phenomena: rural-urban migration and an increase in the ratio of the working population to the dependent population. Both of these phenomena are reaching critical turning points, leading to greater challenges in export growth and low-cost, labor-intensive industrialization. Wages are going up, workers are choosier about employment opportunities, and labor markets are tightening in these key sectors (Cai 2008).

Rural to urban migration in reformed China began in the late 1980s as the government relaxed its strict control over internal migration and residency status through the *hukou* system. *Hukou* is the shorthand term for the broader household registration system, which permits administrative control over China's population. This system, which was established by the People's Republic of China in the 1950s, has connections to earlier forms of population control and registration in the Republican and Imperial periods, but the Chinese Communist Party went much further in administrative control over internal migration, in particular after the Great Leap Forward, 1958–1961, when very severe restrictions on rural to urban migration were put into effect. The *hukou* policy's constraints on migration meant that disparities between rural and urban citizens became entrenched and long lasting. Rural citizens were mostly shut out of employment opportunities in cities. Education became the one sure path out of rural life. (For a general discussion of *hukou* policies and history, see Chan and Buckingham [2008]; Chan and Zhang [1999]; and Wang [2005].)

The relaxation of migration policies that began in the 1980s and quickened in the 1990s restarted the process of rural to urban migration, which is the normal development path for industrializing countries. Rural migration has increased rapidly since then as many young and middle-aged rural residents have left their legal residency in the rural areas to find employment in factories, services, or construction in coastal cities and development zones. The most recent 2010 census estimates that there are now nearly 200 million rural migrants in China. However, many rural citizens still find it difficult to become legal residents of the urban areas where they live and work. This is especially the case for those with low education.

China's growth trajectory has been heavily reliant on this migrant workforce, and its ability to access this rural surplus labor sets China apart from other reforming socialist or postsocialist countries. The large amount of surplus labor in agriculture suppressed the wages of migrant workers continuously during the 1990s and into this century (Yang 2011b). Migrant workers have also been willing to work in exploitative conditions, including very long hours, unsafe environments, and insecure employment. Compared to the urban workers employed in the collective and state sectors, these workers were pliable, with low expectations about pay, conditions, and the terms of employment. Access to this labor pool significantly enhanced China's ability to adopt export-oriented industrialization, following in the steps of its capitalist East Asian neighbors.

This period of rapid industrialization was also aided by the changing structure of the Chinese population as the one-child policy kicked in gradually in the 1970s. Birth rates declined while death rates also declined as people lived longer. There was an important period for growth when the ratio of the working population grew relative to the dependent population. Younger dependents declined faster than the retired population grew (Wang 2011). This period ended in 2010, when China's working population began to decline. Yang (2011a) calls this China's "condensed demographic transition." Compared to other populous developing nations, China's demographic changes are happening faster due to the effects of the one-child policy.

There is considerable debate within and outside China about the nature of the current migrant labor shortage. Some question how it can exist permanently when there are still millions of potential migrants in rural areas (Knight, Deng, and Li 2010). Others note that this labor shortage coexists with equally dramatic reports of unemployment and underemployment of college graduates. I deal with the first issue in the next section. The second issue, on the coexistence of labor shortage and surplus, should be dealt with here.

China's labor markets are highly segmented with continuing institutional barriers to labor mobility across regions and across sectors. The *hukou* system is still fundamental in placing barriers between the labor markets of urban and rural citizens. There are also important social and cultural expectations about employment that further segment labor markets. Unemployed college graduates and unemployed rural migrants rarely compete in the same labor markets. There are some jobs that urban youth simply do not consider. Conversely, few employers in labor-intensive manufacturing would want to hire urban youth, who might not work hard enough or be able to withstand the harsh conditions. The very rapid expansion of the college educated since 2000 means that the requisite jobs for the college elite have not grown as quickly as that elite. Meanwhile, labor intensive manufacturing has grown very rapidly as China gained membership into the World Trade Organization and began to attract investment from other Asian countries that used to export directly to the United States and other developed markets. Barriers to labor mobility and segmentation based on *hukou* status and education level continue to exist in China. These factors help explain how labor shortages and labor surplus can coexist.

THE CHANGING SOCIAL CONTEXT OF THE
"NEW GENERATION" OF MIGRANTS

The one-child policy and the changes to China's internal migration policies have also had transformative effects on the social and cultural characteristics of China's youngest migrants, sometimes called the "new generation of migrants" (新生代农民工) to mark their differences from the earlier generation of migrant workers who left rural China in search of better opportunities after relaxation of the *hukou* system (Qiao and Chen 2010). These differences can be related to their status as part of the first "only child" generation, their better educational opportunities under reform, and their greater exposure to global youth culture through technological expertise and access to more sophisticated communication methods.

Migrant workers born in and after the 1980s are part of a reform generation that is markedly different in basic characteristics, in political socialization, and in life experiences from that of their parents. In terms of basic demography, this generation is the first to be affected by the strict "one-child" policy that was implemented in the late 1970s. While in their parents' generation a family might have several children, even rural children in this generation generally share at most one sibling. In urban areas, the majority of children born are only children. Given their greater importance to the family's economy and long-term success, these "little emperors" have been lavished with attention and opportunity. Even rural children, who do not have the same educational and economic opportunities of their urban counterparts, have been given more attention and more protection from hard agricultural labor than in previous generations. Many rural parents understand that education is still the key to social mobility for their children. This focus on education has spared children backbreaking manual labor and allowed them to focus on their studies. Although rural children do not attain the same level of education as urban children, they now have much higher rates of middle school and high school completion. Even when they move on to labor intensive manufacturing as part of their "going out" strategy, they are already better educated and better prepared to make the transition to urban life. These educational characteristics also indicate the inexperience of post-1980 rural children with agricultural work. An All China Federation of Trade Unions study found that 89 percent of migrant workers in southern China did not intend to ever do agricultural work, and less than 45 percent had ever done it before leaving home (Qiao and Chen 2010).

The post-1980s generation, both rural and urban, is also markedly different from their parents in terms of political socialization and life experiences under socialism. As children of the reform era, they have little familiarity with the mass political campaigns of the high Mao era. Their primary years of education and political socialization coincided with post-Tiananmen China, when economic growth was the major goal and the Chinese Communist Party emphasized a party open to all sectors of society, including entrepreneurs. The private sector was allowed to expand, and the "rule by law" campaign was disseminated in the media, encouraging people to protect their legal rights. The rural-to-urban migration boom is also linked to this time period as China opened further to foreign direct investment and labor-intensive manufacturing development zones multiplied across the coastal provinces.

These different demographic characteristics and life experiences have helped create a new generation of migrants who are challenging traditional barriers and identities that have existed in China since the Maoist *hukou* policy was put into place in the late 1950s. Three main characteristics of this new generation are worth examining here: 1) their frame of reference, 2) their long-term expectations, and 3) their potential capacity to organize their interests and grievances collectively.

As surveys and interviews with young migrants show, young rural migrants are increasingly better integrated and familiar with global youth culture and Chinese urban culture. Their frame of reference is increasingly not what *would* have happened to them if they had stayed in the countryside, but what is possible for them as young, aspiring urban citizens. This change in their reference point (who they want to become) is, of course, related to their long-term plans and expectations. Rural migrants to Chinese cities generally do not envision a return to the countryside, but rather they hope for a gradual personal transformation from a low status to higher status. These aspirations translate into higher expectations on the job and some tendency to value work that offers future opportunity even at the expense of current lower pay. Many migrants also report distaste of jobs that are too lowly, dirty, dangerous, or boring. So, in addition to planning a gradual transition to urban life, migrants also envision a certain degree of social and economic mobility. These expectations shape their workplace choices and, over time, they have become more selective about their place of employment when possible.

Given this generation's higher levels of education, better access to technology, and increased integration into urban culture, there seems to be greater potential for this generation to articulate collective interests and to act collectively to press for their interests and rights, vis-à-vis employers and the government alike. Chinese urban workers have acted collectively in the past, often organized by work unit, to protest about state-owned enterprise restructuring. Rural migrants have also used native-place affiliations and familial bonds to organize, but these modes of organization have not served them well at their urban workplaces where divisions between workers of different origins, dialects, and local cultures can be used by employers to fragment workers' collective identity. In the strikes of 2010, observers pointed to workers' new ability to organize within single workplaces and to design institutions to allow for leadership selection and representation.

A collective identity is also being formed in the media and even in academia with the term *new generation* and the public attention to migrant conditions and social discrimination. This external validation of a collective identity is also a factor in the increased potential for young migrants' collective power. These social changes are not divorced from the changing political context. Since 2003, the party state has been much more attentive to and worried about the conditions and long-term development of China's urbanizing citizens. This is the final context to which we now turn.

THE CHANGING POLITICAL CONTEXT

In 2003, the rising number of labor disputes, large-scale and destabilizing migrant workers' wage arrears problem, and the media uproar over Sun Zhigang (a rural college graduate beaten to death in police custody in Guangzhou) redirected the state to focus on migrant labor issues. There were also a number of positive reasons for the state's decision to begin to protect migrant workers' rights. First, labor unrest that had followed the state-owned enterprise restructuring of 1999–2001 had begun to abate, and the state was feeling more confident about its ability to manage labor unrest through a combination of legal institutions and party-led direct intervention in labor-capital relations. Second, as Chinese growth boomed in the first decade of this century, the central government began to plan a gradual industrial upgrading for the coastal provinces and a move away from dependence on labor-intensive manufacturing. Raising wages, expanding protections, and enhancing employment security were all hoped-for policy consequences, but the government also aspired to draw new manufacturing investment into the central and western provinces, and to alleviate some of the imbalances and regional inequality that had developed alongside rapid growth and reform.

It should also be noted that in addition to these positive or forward-thinking aspects of the policy shift, the party state was and continues to be intently interested in preserving political stability. Positive developments such as increased employment security, new policies for collective wage bargaining, and enhanced position of the trade union are all part of an attempt to limit the development of an independent labor movement that might, in concert with other social forces, pressure the Chinese Communist Party to share power. When enhanced labor rights (or effective implementation of rights already on the books) clash with the imperative of the party's monopoly on political power, labor rights have been trumped.

THE LEGISLATIVE AGENDA: THE LABOR CONTRACT LAW

The Labor Contract Law, which was passed in 2007 and went into effect in 2008, is the paradigmatic example of China's socialist party state regaining its interest in enhanced workers' rights and better employment security. The period of reform from the 1980s through the beginning of the current century marked a gradual but relentless assault on the entitlements and privileges of the urban socialist workforce. Laws, regulations, and special reform measures, such as state enterprise restructuring, were constructed to chip away at the "iron rice bowl" of employment security and extensive social benefits. The Labor Contract Law, through a supplementary law to the more market-friendly 1994 Labor Law of the People's Republic of China, signals a shift from ever-increasing labor market flexibility, informalization, and insecure work (Gallagher and Dong 2011).

In contrast to the basic principles of the Labor Law, the Labor Contract Law has enhanced employment security through more stringent restrictions on (usually short) fixed-term contracts as the foundation of industrial relations in China. It also is more specific in some of the penalties for violations, and it grants the trade union more detailed provisions for collective negotiations. Although most media and academic attention has been on this law, there have been other legislative advances, including the Labor Dispute Mediation and Arbitration Law (2008), the Employment Promotion Law (2007), and the Social Insurance Law (2010). In addition to national level legislation, many localities have responded to the center's push with local legislation and regulations of their own. Because the Labor Contract Law's first year of implementation coincided with the Global Financial Crisis of 2008, however, some localities have attempted to use local implementation to reduce the impact of the Labor Contract Law on enterprises' operational autonomy and the locality's ability to attract external investment (Harper Ho 2009).

THE JUDICIAL AGENDA: MEDIATION ABOVE ALL

The untimely confluence of a new, well-publicized, more protective law; a global economic crisis of unforeseen proportion; and longer-term trends in rising wages and choosier workers led to an explosion of labor disputes in 2008, with these high rates sustained into more recent years. The central government, while committed to the new protections offered by the Labor Contract Law and other related laws, responded to this new spike in disputes with renewed emphasis on mediation and a sustained critique of and departure from adversarial resolution processes, especially litigation. This renewed interest in mediation is part of a broader agenda promoting the construction of a "harmonious society" under the aegis of the Chinese Communist Party. It is a clear promotion of alternative models of political and social representation, away from democracy, pluralism, and freedom of association. While recognizing the need to promote the protection of workers' rights, the party state has no intention of allowing such protection to flow into other areas of political reform.

Mediation of labor disputes has long been enshrined as one method of dispute resolution. In the 1994 Labor Law, mediation is a voluntary first step in the resolution process. In those days, it was expected that mediation would occur within the enterprise and that the enterprise trade union would play a critical middleman role in bringing the two sides to an accepted compromise. With the reform of the state and collective sectors in the 1990s and the expansion of the private and foreign sectors, enterprise mediation declined quite dramatically as workers chose to resolve disputes at higher levels of administration and enterprises no longer maintained internal institutions that could serve in a mediating capacity.

The recent revival of mediation has had to go beyond the enterprise, relying on government and party structures at the grassroots level to ensure harmonious resolution of labor disputes. This has led to some significant pressure on the institutions that manage arbitration and litigation (the labor bureaus and the courts, respectively) to provide ample opportunities and incentives for mediated outcomes. Arbitrators and judges are encouraged through the evaluation systems to reach high levels of mediated settlements. When large collective disputes break out spontaneously at the workplace, the government sends out "stability preservation teams" that use intergovernment and party coordination to pressure workers and employers alike for a mediated outcome (He and Su 2010). While legal experts have decried this trend as part of a larger shift away from "rule by law" (Minzner 2011), the party's return to mediation is not surprising given the historical importance of mediation to resolve "contradictions within the people"—an idea important to Maoist thought (Lubman 1999). It is also a necessary adjustment to the very rapid growth in disputes wrought by the combination of economic changes and a rapidly developing legal system that gives workers impressive rights on paper. As more empowered workers make claims in the courts and in arbitration committees, the state has responded by pushing mediation. The continued reliance on mediation and the state's ambivalence toward some of the consequences of its earlier decision to develop the legal system (more social conflict, more overtly adversarial modes of resolution) are indicative of the contradictions embedded in the Chinese system.

Reliance on mediation requires that the local government play a central role in the resolution of social disputes. It is intended to serve as a substitute for a more pluralistic opening toward effective collective representation of labor and capital. Instead of empowering the actors directly involved in disputes, the state has chosen to implicate itself directly into the resolution process. By doing so, the state can carefully push for better protection of workers' interests while ensuring that worker demands do not grow too strong and threaten the local economy, or morph into political demands that might challenge the Chinese Communist Party's hold on power.

THE INSTITUTIONAL AGENDA: COLLECTIVE WAGE BARGAINING AND MANAGED INDUSTRIAL TRANSFORMATION

The Chinese state's laser focus on "preserving social stability" (维稳) is always to maintain the political status quo, which allows the Chinese economy to continue to grow and the Chinese state to grow wealthier and more powerful. It builds up extremely important domestic and international legitimacy. But the Chinese state is nothing if not extremely ambitious. China's leaders realize that maintaining the status quo is not enough; stability is the prerequisite for other plans.

In this context of needing to maintain economic growth, but also to fix long-term problems, such as rising inequality and economic imbalances, the Chinese state envisions a gradual process of industrial transformation from labor-intensive manufacturing to high-tech, capital-intensive manufacturing and research and development. China's role as the workshop of the world is a stepping-stone to something more valuable—as the laboratory of the world, as the R&D center of the world. At the same time, the movement of labor-intensive manufacturing from the coastal development zones of Guangdong and Jiangsu to internal provinces such as Henan, Sichuan, and Jiangxi will begin to alleviate China's dramatic regional inequality. It will also make the urbanization of China's rural workers more tractable. Instead of leaving home to seek out urban areas for employment and opportunity, China's rural citizens will have the jobs come to them. China's new urban citizens will live in newly created cities as farms become suburbs and suburbs become metropolitan centers in their own right.

One challenge revealed by the 2010 automotive strikes that has not been solved by the heavy-handed push for mediation and the new legal protections is the lack of institutional capacity for labor-capital bargaining around interest conflicts. The vast majority of the nearly 700,000 labor disputes in 2009 are "rights disputes," when there is a conflict about the violation of the labor laws themselves. However, Chinese workers and employers have many disagreements and conflicts about their interests, such as wage increases, working conditions, quality of the cafeteria food, or the transportation from workplace to home. Many of the striking automotive workers in 2010, for example, were motivated by a desire for wage increases that reduced the wage inequality between Japanese and Chinese workers employed by the same company and between Chinese workers in different plants owned by the same company. Because in most cases their wages already exceeded the minimum wage standards for their locality, they had wage demands that could not be settled through the current process of labor dispute resolution, which can only handle disputes over rights.

Since the 2010 strikes, the government has revived the idea that China needs a system of collective bargaining and negotiation that would allow for regular and systematic discussion about wages between the government, employers, and workers. Such a system, it is believed, would not only reduce the likelihood of spontaneous workplace actions, but would also contribute to China's desire for industrial transformation. Rising wages will gradually push some employers off the coast toward China's central and western provinces, where incomes and expectations are much lower. The coastal provinces, with higher levels of education, a developed transportation infrastructure, and well-established ties to global production networks, will lead China in its next reformist effort, toward a knowledge economy. Like most development paradigms, this is a utopian vision, the realization of which is not assured. But it puts into better context the underlying reasons for the government's support for more protective labor laws and the painstaking balance it strives to maintain between gains for labor (improved working conditions and enhanced representation) and social stability, continued economic growth, and political dictatorship.

CONCLUSION

This chapter has attempted to place China's recent labor activism into the broader context of China's development trajectory. As noted in the three areas discussed above—demography, society, and politics—recent trends of increased labor activism cannot be explained by any one dimension, but rather by the confluence of factors that are currently in alignment. This alignment has widened the political space available to workers in pushing for new demands. Tighter labor markets have focused the minds of employers who had grown used to low expectations and a labor surplus. Political leaders at the top have realized that in order to rectify the dramatic growth in inequality since the 1980s, China's coastal provinces must yield investment to cheaper places inland. China's political system, however, has not changed, and there is no sign of any opening for freedom of association, independent unions, or a truly worker-led labor movement. The Chinese Communist Party hopes that it will satisfy the needs and demands of the new generation of workers, and in doing so make a workers' movement against the party itself unnecessary.

References

Cai, Fang. 2008. "Approaching a Triumphal Span: How Far Is China toward Its Lewisian Turning Point?" Research Paper No. 2008/09. World Institute for Development Economics Research. Helsinki, Finland: World Institute for Development Economics Research, United Nations University.

Cai, Fang, and Meiyan Wang. 2011. "Chinese Wages and the Turning Point in the Chinese Economy." East Asia Forum, January 29. http://www.eastasiaforum.org/2011/01/29/chinese-wages-and-the-turning-point-in-the-chinese-economy (accessed January 5, 2012).

Chan, Kam Wing, and Will Buckingham. 2008. "Is China Abolishing the Hukou System?" China Quarterly 195: 582–606.

Chan, Kam Wing, and Li Zhang. 1999. "The Hukou System and Rural-Urban

Migration in China: Processes and Changes." *China Quarterly* 160: 818–855.

Gallagher, Mary E., and Dong Baohua. 2011. "Legislating Harmony: Labor Law Reform in Contemporary China." In *From Iron Rice Bowl to Informalization: Markets, Workers, and the State in a Changing China*, Sarosh Kuruvilla, Ching Kwan Lee, and Mary Gallagher, eds. Ithaca, NY: Cornell University Press, pp. 36–60.

Harper Ho, Virginia E. 2009. "From Contracts to Compliance? An Early Look at Implementation under China's New Labor Legislation." *Columbia Journal of Asian Law* 23(1): 34.

He, Xin, and Yang Su. 2010. "Street as Courtroom: State Accommodation of Labor Protests in South China." *Law and Society Review* 44(1): 157–185.

Knight, John, Deng Quheng, and Li Shi. 2010. "The Puzzle of Migrant Labour Shortage and the Rural Labour Surplus in China." Department of Economics Working Paper Series No. 494. Oxford: University of Oxford.

Lubman, Stanley. 1999. *Bird in a Cage: Legal Reform in China after Mao*. Stanford, CA: Stanford University Press.

Minzner, Carl. 2011. "China's Turn against Law." *American Journal of Comparative Law* 59(4): 935–984.

Qiao, Zhuanxiu, and Songshu Chen. 2010. "Research Report on the Problems of the New Generation of Migrant Workers." Unpublished report. http://news.xinhuanet.com/politics/2010-06/21/c_12240721.htm (in Chinese, accessed July 31, 2012).

Wang, Fei-ling. 2005. *Organizing through Exclusion and Division: China's Hukou System.* Stanford, CA: Stanford University Press.

Wang, Feng. 2011. "The Future of a Demographic Overachiever: Long-Term Implications of the Demographic Transition in China." *Population and Development Review* 37(Supplement): 173–190.

Yang, Yao. 2011a. "The Relationship between China's Export-Led Growth and Its Double Transition of Demographic Change and Industrialization." *Asian Economic Papers* 10(2): 52–76.

———. 2011b. "China's Export-Led Growth Model." East Asia Forum, February 27. http://www.eastasiaforum.org/2011/02/27/chinas-export-led-growth-model/ (accessed January 5, 2012).

6
Left Behind in Old Age?

Sources of Support for China's Rural Elderly in a Period of Growth, Migration, and Demographic Transition

John Giles

World Bank and the Institute for Labor

Over the last 25 years, average incomes have risen considerably as China's economy has undergone unprecedented growth and dramatic reductions in poverty. Not all regions of the country have benefited uniformly (Benjamin et al. 2008; Ravallion and Chen 2007) as gaps have grown between coastal and interior regions and between urban and rural areas of the country (Kanbur and Zhang 1999, 2005). In addition to geographic poverty traps that lead to different patterns of income and consumption growth (Jalan and Ravallion 2002), there are also considerable differences across demographic groups not only in income levels (Chaudhuri and Datt 2009), but also in the level of coverage by safety nets and in the risks of falling into poverty (Duclos, Araar, and Giles 2010; Jalan and Ravallion 1999). In particular, the movement of young rural adults to urban and coastal areas for higher income earning opportunities raises the prospect that older residents remaining in rural areas are at greater risk of falling into poverty. In general, rural residents lack access to pension support when they are of retirement age, and must rely on either their own labor income or support from family members, even as they age into their 70s and beyond. In rural China, financial support for the elderly remains the responsibility of adult children and is even codified into laws governing the family (Marriage Law 2001). As the population of potential care providers continues to shrink as a result of both China's demographic transition and the availability of attractive migrant employment opportunities for the young, many observers have expressed concerns for the well-being of the rural elderly (Benjamin,

Brandt, and Rozelle 2000; Jiang and Zhao 2009; Li, Lu, and Feldman 2009; Yao 2006).

In this chapter, I use the 2005 1 percent population sample to document the sources of support for older rural residents, and then present updated evidence on the rates both at which the rural elderly coreside with adult children and live in proximity to them. I then provide descriptive evidence on the extent to which private net transfers from adult children respond to low income levels of their elderly parents. To do this, I first introduce a framework for examining how net transfers respond to elderly income, and then make use of a unique data source with information on the age and residence location of all nonresident children of the household. These features of the data source allow us to reduce one form of bias common in many studies of intergenerational transfers: we control for the size and quality of the transfer network. Given specific concerns over abandonment by adult children, I examine whether transfer responsiveness varies when an elderly person has migrant children, and moreover, whether the variance of expected transfers differs between elderly with migrant children and those who only have children living nearby.

The descriptive evidence presented shows somewhat higher variance in the predicted transfers to the elderly who have migrant children, which is consistent with concerns that the current and future elderly may face more uncertainty in their support. Given that migrants employed in nonagricultural work are frequently in the informal sector, their incomes often are much more risky, thus it is not surprising that this risk is reflected in transfers to their parents. To decrease risk to private transfer income, China's government is currently supporting new rural pension programs that are designed to reduce these perceived risks of elderly poverty and to complement existing motives for private transfers.

Apart from income support from the family, income from own labor remains the other important source of support for the rural elderly. Recent research on elderly labor supply provides evidence that China's rural elderly continue to work well beyond age 60 out of necessity. Recent studies of the retirement decision in rural China suggest that China's rural elderly "work until they drop" (Pang, de Brauw, and Rozelle 2004), and only stop working when physically incapacitated. Physical labor in agriculture can take a significant toll on the bodies of those still working after 60 years of age and raise the likelihood of serious injury. Pension support for the rural elderly can be expected to have a significant impact on the importance of working into old age, and is likely to affect the labor supply decisions of the elderly. One benefit of a rural pension is that it could make retirement a feasible choice, and thus improve standards of living of the rural elderly.

In this chapter, I document the labor supply patterns of the rural elderly and show that a considerable share of that population works well beyond age 70. I examine the effects of both adult child migration and increasing family wealth on labor supply decisions of the elderly. The potential benefit that a pension may play in facilitating retirement is evident as I observe declining labor supply with increases in family wealth and other sources of income.

The following section of the chapter presents evidence on the sources of support among China's rural elderly. It first presents descriptive statistics from the 2005 1 percent population sample on sources of support for China's elderly, with particular attention to contrasts between elderly living in rural and urban areas, and then discusses implications of changes in living arrangements that underscore concerns that the rural elderly are at increasing risk of falling into poverty. Finally, the section presents evidence on the responsiveness of transfers to the income levels of elderly households, with attention to changes in responsiveness over time. As the rural elderly often support themselves through work relatively late in life, the following section presents evidence on the determinants of elderly labor supply. In particular, it highlights the relationships between income, health, and migrant status of children and labor supply of men and women in their 60s and 70s. A final section summarizes important findings.

SOURCES OF SUPPORT AMONG CHINA'S RURAL ELDERLY

Major differences exist in the primary sources of support for China's urban and rural elderly and between men and women from both groups of elderly. Table 6.1 presents findings on elderly sources of support by location and gender for 2005. Several differences across groups

Table 6.1 Primary Source of Support for China's Elderly, 2005 (%)

Source of support	Urban			Rural		
	Average	Male	Female	Average	Male	Female
Labor income	13.0	18.4	7.9	37.9	48.5	27.5
Pensions	45.4	56.9	34.6	4.6	8.1	1.3
Dibao	2.4	1.8	2.9	1.3	1.8	0.9
Insurance and subsidy	0.3	0.3	0.2	0.1	0.2	0.0
Property income	0.5	0.5	0.5	0.2	0.2	0.1
Family support	37.0	20.7	52.3	54.1	39.3	68.5
Other	1.5	1.4	1.6	1.8	2.0	1.7

NOTE: Most significant share of support reported.
SOURCE: National Bureau of Statistics (2006).

among the elderly are notable. First, although pensions are the single most significant source of support for the urban elderly, they remain a very minor source of support for the rural elderly, almost entirely confined to former civil servants and soldiers, and former village cadres.[1] In contrast, labor income is a much more significant source of support for the rural elderly than for the urban elderly, being the primary source of support for 37.9 percent of the rural elderly. Family support is an important primary support for both rural and urban elderly households, but its role for the rural elderly is substantially greater.

Support through antipoverty programs does not figure prominently, most likely because the rural *dibao*—a social aid program providing cash assistance to the rural poor—was not an important source of income support for rural or urban elderly households.[2] This finding may stem from the fact that the rural *dibao* was still being phased in at the time of the survey, although policy has shifted in the intervening period with the approval of rural *dibao* as national policy in 2007 with a resultant expansion in coverage.[3] Also notable is the inability of the elderly to earn income from property. In contrast to member countries of the Organisation for Economic Co-operation and Development historically or other developing countries today, the elderly in China have not grown old in an environment in which they could accumulate land wealth. Lack of land wealth limits the ability of the elderly to earn income from rents and may also limit the scope for encouraging intergenerational transfers from their children (who would be prospective heirs).

Looking at sources of support by gender among the rural elderly, family support is more important for elderly women and labor income remains more important for men. As shown in Table 6.1, 68.5 percent of women over 60 report that financial support from family members is their most important source of support, whereas only 27.5 percent report that labor income is most important. By contrast, 48.5 percent of elderly men report that labor income remains their most important source of support; only 39.3 percent report support from family members. When distinguishing the importance of pension by gender, a significantly higher share of rural men (8.1 percent) than women (1.3 percent) report that pension income is their most significant source of financial support. The gap between men and women reflects historical differences between genders in employment in local government and the military.

Rural elderly in their 60s are more likely to support themselves through labor income, whereas those over 70 depend far more on support from family members. Table 6.2 shows results by age cohort among the rural elderly and emphasizes the differences in financial support between younger and older elderly people. Younger elderly rely more on labor income, and a shift starts after age 70. Notably, however, nearly a quarter of the elderly between 70 and 75 report labor income as their main source of support. Apart from family support and labor income, no other source of support for the elderly varies significantly by age group. Moreover, no other component plays a particularly significant role.

Table 6.2 Source of Support for China's Rural Elderly, by Age Group in 2005 (share of income in percent)

Source of support	Age group (years)						
	60+	60–64	65–69	70–74	75–79	80–84	85+
Labor income	37.9	64.3	45.1	24.4	12.0	4.3	1.7
Pensions	4.6	4.7	5.1	4.7	4.4	3.8	2.6
Dibao	1.3	0.8	1.2	1.5	1.9	2.0	2.1
Insurance and subsidy	0.1	0.1	0.1	0.1	0.1	0.1	0.1
Property income	0.2	0.1	0.2	0.2	0.2	0.1	0.1
Family support	54.1	28.6	46.6	66.9	79.1	87.2	91.1
Other	1.8	1.2	1.7	2.2	2.3	2.4	2.3

SOURCE: National Bureau of Statistics (2006).

Evidence on Family Support

Until the last few years, policy on pensions and safety nets has not focused significantly on the rural elderly because the family was assumed to be an adequate source of support. Policymakers had assumed the continued viability of traditional, family-based arrangements for two reasons. First, family values remain strong in rural areas, and Confucian filial piety continues to sustain family care for the elderly. Second, any formal public policy response to the needs of the rural elderly may undermine existing private arrangements. For example, state transfers to the elderly may crowd out existing transfers from younger family members.

With regard to the reliance on traditional family values, both policymakers and other observers have in recent years questioned the view that family support for the rural elderly will be sufficient. Fertility decline driven by China's population policies may ultimately lead to a breakdown of the traditional support system, but conclusions from research spanning the literature on demography and economics disagree on the likeliness of this outcome. Zimmer and Kwong (2003) show that more children increase the likelihood that the elderly will receive support, but current simulation results suggest that declines in fertility alone will not lead to a collapse of family-based support for the elderly. Other research has suggested that financial transfers to parents respond to low income and low health status in urban areas (Cai, Giles, and Meng 2006), but that in rural areas interhousehold transfers are not often observed because they take the form of labor input into family farming (Lee and Xiao 1998).[4] The following sections provide empirical evidence on elderly living arrangements and responsiveness of financial support to low incomes.

Recent Changes to Living Arrangements and the Well-Being of the Elderly

The share of rural elderly living with their children has declined rapidly, both in the long term and in recent years. Changes in living arrangements have been cited most frequently as a reason for concern for the well-being of the elderly. For example, Benjamin, Brandt, and Rozelle (2000) note that in rural northern China, over 85 percent of the elderly lived in extended households in 1935, but this figure had dropped to just over 60 percent by 1995.[5] The decline in coresidence with adult children is strikingly evident over the six rounds of the China Health and Nutrition Survey from 1991 to 2006. Figure 6.1 shows that in the survey, nearly 70 percent of elderly in rural areas lived with an adult child in 1991, but by 2006 this share had fallen to just over 40 percent. As elderly parent age increases, the probability of coresidence with an adult child approaches 100 percent.[6]

At the same time, a decline in coresidence does not necessarily reflect a drop in provision of care to the elderly. In-kind transfers, such as supply of labor on extended family plots, are difficult to pick up in surveys, yet such transfers often occur both within and across households. Changes in living arrangements reflect the increasing wealth of families. With increasing resources, coresidence may be unnecessary in caring for the elderly. Within villages in rural areas, elders and adult children are typically in the same small group (a sub-village administrative unit) and live in proximity to one another. Given increases in housing wealth in rural areas since the mid-1980s, the trend toward nuclear

Figure 6.1 Living Arrangements of China's Rural Elderly

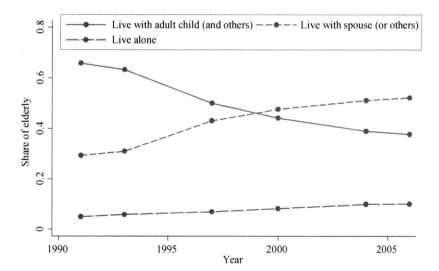

SOURCE: China Health and Nutrition Survey (1991, 1993, 1997, 2000, 2004, 2006).

families may signal a wealth effect independent of the traditional value of providing support and care to elderly parents.

In addition, the share of rural elderly with an adult child living nearby was actually higher. A more important factor may be the proximity of adult children, not whether they coreside. Figure 6.2 summarizes the living arrangements by age cohort from the 2004 Research Center for Rural Economy (RCRE) supplemental survey and includes information on children living within the same village as their elders. Although coresidence with adult children was less than 60 percent during the 2003 reference period among those 60–70 years of age, more than half the elderly living alone or with a spouse in this age range had at least one adult child living in the village.[7] This finding suggests that even though coresidence was well below the levels of the 1930s, adult children were still potentially available to provide care.

Evidence suggests that migration decisions of adult children are influenced by the well-being of elderly parents. Decline in coresidence reflects a decline in support for the elderly only if associated with increased abandonment of the elderly. The rural elderly may have suf-

Figure 6.2 Living Arrangements of China's Rural Elderly, by Age

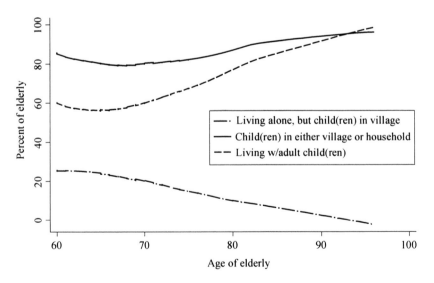

SOURCE: Giles and Mu (2007).

ficient support if they are receiving transfers from local or migrant adult children. Giles and Mu (2007) explore this possibility by conducting separate analyses using two different data sources. They find a significantly lower probability that a son will work as a migrant when a parent is seriously ill. Although parental illness has a statistically significant effect on migration, it does not completely drive the decision to return from migrant destinations. Depending on the data set and methodology, the effect of illness varied from a 15 percent to 26 percent reduction in the probability that a son would be employed as a migrant, and this effect was reduced if other siblings remained behind in the village. Although this level of responsiveness to elderly illness is significant, it is not absolute. Moreover, elderly who are relatively healthy may have a much lower standard of living if nonresident adult children who are migrants are less likely to make transfers to their parents than adult children who live nearby. In light of these findings, the next section examines how private transfers respond to low income levels of the elderly, including whether transfer responsiveness differs with migrant status of children.

Do Private Transfers Respond to Income of the Elderly?

Two important reasons exist to examine the responsiveness of transfers and transfer levels. First, as China rolls out its national rural pension program, concerns may arise about formal support for the elderly crowding out transfers from private sources. Second, while evidence from the risk-coping literature suggests that elderly households with migrant family members may be less likely to fall into poverty (Cai et al. 2012; Giles 2006), these findings are average effects and do not explore how transfers vary with pretransfer household income, nor do they consider the distribution of transfers and the risks that the elderly may fall into poverty if transfers do not materialize.

Much early research on intrafamily transfers had used data from developed countries and focused on efforts to distinguish whether transfers were motivated by altruistic or exchange motives.[8] This distinction is important as it has implications for how transfers respond to exogenous income received by elderly households. If an altruistic motive dominates, then family members outside the household may respond to reduced levels of income by providing an offsetting transfer. This raises the possibility that any increase in income, as might occur with a noncontributory pension payment, would lead to an offsetting reduction in transfers into the household. If the altruistic motive dominates, the transfer derivative (which picks up responsiveness of transfers to income) will have an unambiguously negative sign and the magnitude will equal one if increased income perfectly crowds out private transfers. When exchange motives or other motives are more important, then we are unlikely to observe any crowding out with increased incomes, and the transfer derivative may not be significantly different from zero.

Policy research examining the motives for transfers in developing countries has emphasized the importance of allowing both altruistic and exchange motives to be present at different levels of income. Theory thus suggests a net transfer function for the elderly:

$$(6.1) \quad T_i^N = f(I_i) + \mathbf{X}_i'\gamma + \varepsilon_i,$$

where T_i^N are net transfers into the household, I_i is a measure of pretransfer income, and X_i is a vector of other exogenous variables which influence levels of transfers into and out of the household (and γ is the corresponding vector of coefficients on X_i). Errors in measurement and unexplained sources of variation are then represented by ε_i. What is important in this model is that we allow pretransfer income, I_i, to have a nonlinear effect on net transfer responses. Estimating how net transfers, T_i^N, vary with pretransfer income is our primary objective, but to do this we must appropriately control for other factors, X_i, that affect transfers into the household.

Our choice of data source to use for this analysis is driven by concern that omitted variables related to the potential transfer network outside the household could bias estimates of how transfers respond to pretransfer income. This would occur, for example, if the size or quality of the transfer network was systematically related to pretransfer income. If number of children or their ability (measured through education) also reflects unmeasured dimensions of the ability of household members, then this may well be the case. In addition, knowing whether a household has family members who have migrated, even if in the more distant past, is important for making comparisons across households with migrant children and those with family members living locally.

The most appropriate existing data source for the study of transfer behavior is the RCRE household survey complemented with a Supplemental Survey conducted in RCRE households in 2004.[9] An important feature of the survey is that it enumerated characteristics of former household members, including their current location and educational attainment, and this allows us to control for both the size and quality of the transfer network. Thus, among the regressors influencing the size of transfers, we include the number of children, which captures the effect of the potential transfer network size, and average education of children living outside the household, which proxies for the quality of the transfer network.[10]

Arguing that $f(I_i)$ may be nonlinear due to a switch from altruistic to exchange motives for transfers at a particular threshold, Cox, Hansen, and Jimenez (2004) estimate transfer responsiveness using an approach that allows one to estimate this threshold empirically as well. Understanding where this threshold is relative to the poverty line or an eligibility line for minimum living standard support may be important for thinking about safety net design and could be quite useful. Yet, an empirical approach that forces $f(I_i)$ to be composed of two linear portions below and above a threshold may also be too restrictive. Earlier work examining transfers to elderly living in urban China raises doubt about the viability of the threshold model approach. Cai, Giles, and Meng (2006) show that the threshold model introduced by Cox, Hansen, and Jimenez (2004) leads to a switch from altruistic motives at less than half the basic needs poverty line for urban China. While this shouldn't disqualify the approach altogether, the threshold also failed to fit the data very well.

Another approach to allowing $f(I_i)$ to be nonlinear is to use a partial linear model for empirical estimation, and then empirically calculate transfer derivatives at different levels of I_i. We use the partial linear model introduced by Yatchew (2003) and implemented for analysis of transfers in Cai, Giles, and Meng (2006). In this approach, observations in the sample are first ranked by I_i, and then differenced to obtain

(6.2) $\quad \Delta T_i^N = \Delta f(I_i) + \Delta \mathbf{X}_i' \gamma + \Delta \varepsilon_i$.

Since I_i is bounded as the sample size increases, $\Delta f(I_i) \approx 0$, and Equation (6.2) reduces to

(6.3) $\Delta T_i^N = \Delta \mathbf{X}_i' \gamma + \Delta \varepsilon_i$.

As long as I_i and other independent variables are not perfectly correlated, OLS estimation of Equation (6.3) will yield consistent estimates
of γ. In order to estimate the nonparametric relationship $f(I_i)$, we use
the estimated coefficients, $\hat{\gamma}$, to calculate

(6.4) $u_i = T_i^N - \mathbf{X}_i' \hat{\gamma} = f(I_i) + \varepsilon_i$.

Assuming that the ε_i are independent across households and identi-
cally distributed, u_i converges to $f(I_i)$ for large sample sizes. We then
use locally weighted regression (lowess) to estimate the nonparametric relationship between the response of transfers, $f(I_i)$, to pretransfer
income, I_i.[11] We also calculate the income-varying transfer derivatives
of $f(I_i)$ as the slope of $f(I_i)$ in the neighborhood of $[I_i - 100, I_i + 100]$.

In Figure 6.3, we show the estimated transfer response, $f(I_i)$, for
different levels of pretransfer income, I_i. It is likely that transfer responsiveness from migrants may change as time away from home villages
increases.[12] In order to highlight changes in transfer responsiveness
over time, we split the sample into an early period (1995–1998) and a
later period (2000–2003). In each figure, we also separately show how
transfers respond to pretransfer income levels for elderly households
that have migrant children and those that do not. In order to highlight
how transfers respond to income at different points in the income distribution, we draw vertical lines at multiples of an annual nutrition-based
poverty line of 875 RMB yuan per capita, and then report the slopes
calculated at these points in Table 6.3.

Evident in the top panel of Figure 6.3, elderly households found
transfers more responsive to income at low levels in the earlier period
if they had migrant children than if they did not. Indeed, the slope,
or transfer derivative, was not indistinguishable from negative one
for elderly households with pretransfer income below one half of a
nutrition-based poverty line. This suggests that public transfers to the
elderly with migrant children would crowd out private transfers at very
low levels of income. By income levels near the poverty line, however, the transfer derivative was −0.5 for elderly households regardless
of whether or not they had migrant children. Thus, even in the earlier
period, one would not expect private transfers to be crowded out by

Figure 6.3 Net Transfers Received by Rural Elderly, by Migrant Status
of Adult Children

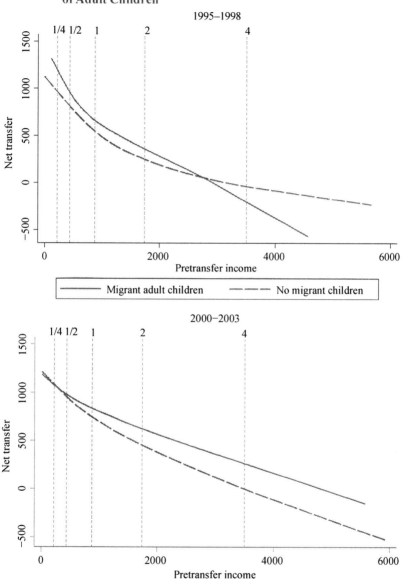

NOTE: Vertical lines indicate multiples of a nutrition-based poverty line, which is equal
to 875 RMB yuan per capita in year 2000 RMB.
SOURCE: Giles, Wang, and Zhao (2010), estimated using data from RCRE Rural
Household Surveys for 1995–2003 from Anhui, Henan, Jiangsu, and Shanxi prov-
inces and the matched RCRE 2004 Supplemental Rural Household Social Network,
Labor Allocation, and Land Use Survey.

Table 6.3 Estimated Transfer Derivatives for Households with Elderly Residents

Estimates in neighborhood of multiples of the poverty line

Multiple	Income per capita (RMB)	Households without migrant children		Households with migrant children	
		1996–98	2000–03	1996–98	2000–03
One-quarter poverty line	119–319	−0.84	−0.67	−1.73	−0.63
One-half poverty line	338–538	−0.73	−0.57	−1.03	−0.35
Poverty line	775–975	−0.52	−0.46	−0.49	−0.25
Twice poverty line	1,650–1,850	−0.28	−0.35	−0.40	−0.21
Four times poverty line	3,400–3,600	−0.11	−0.24	−0.31	−0.20

NOTE: All values are in 2000 RMB yuan per capita. The nutrition-based poverty line is equal to 875 RMB yuan per capita.

SOURCE: Giles, Wang, and Zhao (2010) estimates based on RCRE Rural Household Surveys for 1995–2003 from Anhui, Henan, Jiangsu, and Shanxi provinces and the matched RCRE 2004 Supplemental Rural Household Social Network, Labor Allocation, and Land Use Survey.

payments from a noncontributory pension in those elderly households already at or above the poverty line.

By the later period, we find that private net transfers into households with elderly residents become less responsive to income for households with migrant children. This decline in transfer responsiveness holds for the significant share of households with incomes ranging from half the nutrition-based poverty line (or 438 RMB/capita) to twice this value (or 1750 RMB/capita), and indicates that any concern about a noncontributory pension crowding out private transfers is becoming less relevant over time. Indeed, the decline in responsiveness of transfers to low income raises the possibility that the elderly may be more exposed to the risk of poverty with increases in out-migration of adult children and increasing likelihood that migration of children is permanent.

Will Private Transfers Keep the Rural Elderly Out of Poverty?

When we examine the responsiveness of transfers to pretransfer income above, it is important to remember that the predicted transfer levels in Figure 6.3 should be interpreted as expected values, and that actual transfers will be some distribution around these predicted values. In order to assess the risk that private transfers are not sufficient to keep the elderly out of poverty, we use a bootstrap estimation procedure to estimate the distribution of transfers around the predicted values. In Figure 6.4, we reproduce the predicted transfers from Figure 6.3 with confidence intervals added, and we also plot the threshold of combinations of pretransfer income and private transfers sufficient to keep elderly households above the nutrition-based poverty threshold. This threshold is represented in each of the four graphs of Figure 6.4 as the straight line running from the net transfer axis when pretransfer income is zero to the point on the pretransfer income axis where net transfers are −500 RMB/capita and the household pretransfer income is just sufficient to keep the household out of poverty. The top two panels show the range of net transfers for different levels of pretransfer income during the 1995–1998 period for households without and with migrants, respectively. Comparing the top two figures, note that more of the lower bound of transfers lies below the poverty threshold for households that do not have migrant family members. Indeed, during the earlier period, elderly households with migrant family members appear very unlikely to have income per capita below the poverty line after private transfers are included in household income.

Evident in the fourth panel of Figure 6.4, households with migrant family members are actually at a greater risk of falling into poverty by the 2000–2003 period. The fact that transfers are less responsive to low incomes, as highlighted above, suggests that a noncontributory pension or other support mechanism is unlikely to crowd out private transfers. Figure 6.4 provides evidence that such a transfer may be useful for reducing the risk that elderly households will fall into poverty.

In Table 6.4, we summarize the range of transfers at five multiples of the poverty line. Drawing values from Figure 6.4, evidence summarized in this table suggests that elderly households with pretransfer income per capita less than one-half the nutrition-based poverty line are at particular risk of falling into poverty.

The analysis of transfers presented here suggests that a noncontributory pension has the potential to play an important role in reducing the risk of elderly households falling into poverty. While the rural *dibao* is intended to assist poor households, it only comes into play

Figure 6.4 Confidence Intervals for Net Transfers Received by the Rural Elderly, by Migrant Status of Adult Children

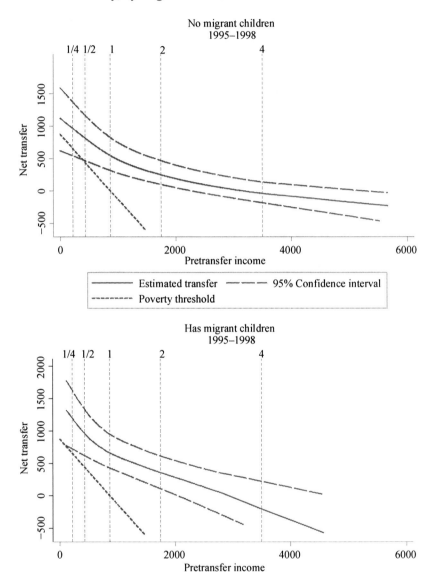

Figure 6.4 (continued)

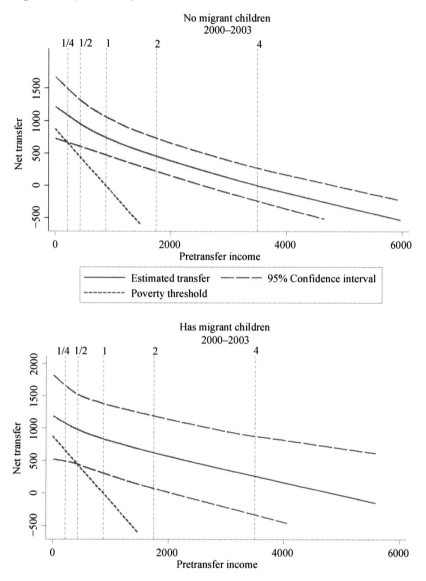

NOTE: Vertical lines indicate multiples of a nutrition-based poverty line, which is equal to 875 RMB yuan per capita in 2000 RMB.

SOURCE: Giles, Wang, and Zhao (2010), estimated using data from RCRE Rural Household Surveys for 1995–2003 from Anhui, Henan, Jiangsu, and Shanxi provinces and the matched RCRE 2004 Supplemental Rural Household Social Network, Labor Allocation, and Land Use Survey.

Table 6.4 Estimated Range of Transfers to Households with Elderly Residents, Results for Neighborhoods of Different Multiples of the Poverty Line

Multiple	Pretransfer income per capita	Portion of estimated range	1995–98		2000–03	
			Households without migrant children	Households with migrant children	Households without migrant children	Households with migrant children
One-quarter poverty line	119–319	Upper bound	1,356	1,643	1,489	1,655
		Mean	948	1,216	1,081	1,071
		Lower bound	531	718	664	479
One-half poverty line	338–538	Upper bound	1,155	1,276	1,293	1,484
		Mean	811	910	942	953
		Lower bound	469	610	601	461
Poverty line	775–975	Upper bound	785	908	1,019	1,381
		Mean	517	648	709	821
		Lower bound	307	420	473	290
Two times poverty line	1,650–1,850	Upper bound	421	605	701	1192
		Mean	212	369	433	615
		Lower bound	87	120	216	55
Four times poverty line	3,400–3,600	Upper bound	125	216	259	862
		Mean	−48	−137	−7	274
		Lower bound	−185	−568	−249	−345

NOTE: All values are in 2000 RMB yuan per capita. The nutrition-based poverty line is equal to 875 RMB yuan per capita.
SOURCE: Giles, Wang, and Zhao (2010) estimates based on RCRE Rural Household Surveys for 1995–2003 from Anhui, Henan, Jiangsu, and Shanxi provinces and the matched RCRE 2004 Supplemental Rural Household Social Network, Labor Allocation, and Land Use Survey.

after a household has been recognized as poor. Lowering the risk that an elderly household falls into poverty can have beneficial effects on a range of economic decisions. In particular, by reducing the risk of falling into poverty, it is likely that the incentive for unproductive forms of precautionary saving are reduced and we are also likely to affect labor supply and retirement decisions of elderly households.

When considering the results from the four-province analysis of transfers, one should remember that although poorer areas of Anhui, Shanxi, and Henan are included in the analysis sample, these provinces are generally considered middle income, and Jiangsu is included among upper-income coastal provinces. If transfer responsiveness to low income is also declining among households with migrant children in poorer regions of China, then a higher share of elderly households are likely to be at risk of slipping into poverty.

THE LABOR SUPPLY AND "RETIREMENT" DECISIONS OF CHINA'S RURAL ELDERLY

Recent studies of retirement decisions in rural China suggest that rural elderly "work until they drop" and stop working only when physically incapacitated (Pang, de Brauw, and Rozelle 2004). Benjamin, Brandt, and Fan (2003) find evidence suggesting that the likelihood of working in agriculture declines significantly with increases in family wealth, raising the possibility that public transfers might facilitate reduced labor supply of the rural elderly. In China's urban areas, where many of the elderly rely on pension support, relatively few elderly continue to work in retirement. By contrast, our earlier discussion noted that nearly 50 percent of rural men and 28 percent of women over retirement age state that income from work remains their primary source of support. Because a considerable number of elderly receiving family support also continue to work, these figures significantly understate the degree to which China's rural elderly continue to work after retirement age.

Even as family wealth and incomes have increased among households in rural China, some data sources suggest that China's rural elderly were more likely to work. Evident in Figure 6.5, employment

Figure 6.5 Employment Status of the Rural Elderly over Time

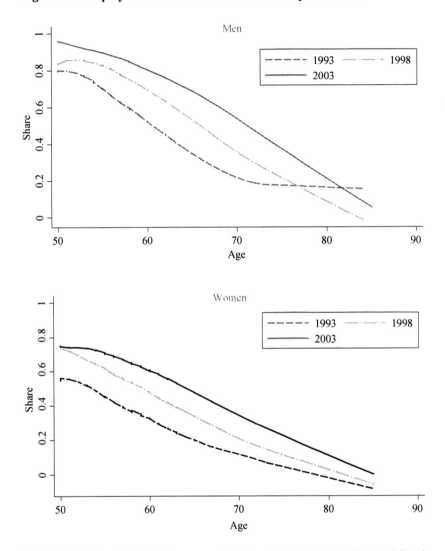

SOURCE: Cai et al. (2012) using survey data from RCRE 2004 Supplemental Rural Household Social Network, Labor Allocation, and Land Use Survey.

status increases across the age distribution from 1993 to 2003 for elderly relatives of RCRE panel households.[13] Indeed, over this period of rising household incomes, employment rates of the rural elderly increased at every age. In fact, continued employment of the elderly may be an important contributing factor to the rising incomes of rural households. As rural household incomes increase with the migrant employment of younger adults, older parents remain behind and continue farming the household land.

Features of China's land tenure system may contribute to the effect of child migration on the labor supply of the elderly. Access to land in rural China has long been the safety net for able-bodied rural residents, but restrictions on the ability to transfer land may also influence the labor supply decisions of rural residents. The inability to rent land further reduces the income of an elderly person in retirement, and the possibility that village leaders will reallocate land that is not kept productive may create additional incentives for older farmers to continue working household land. Changes in the Land Law enacted in 2002 and 2003 may have facilitated land transfer and presumably may also have influenced the labor supply decisions of older rural residents.

To examine the possibility that migration of children is systematically related to labor supply decisions of the elderly, Figure 6.6 shows the share of age cohorts employed by migrant status for men and women in 1998 and 2003. No systematic relationship between elderly retirement and migration status of children is immediately evident. At the same time, however, migration status of children and the labor supply decision of an elderly household resident are both systematically related to household composition, family wealth, earning ability of family members, and health status of the elderly person in question. In order to better characterize the relationship between migration and retirement and labor supply decisions of the elderly, it is important to explicitly model the labor supply decision of the elderly while controlling for these other factors.

As a framework for understanding the retirement and work-intensity decisions of the elderly, assume that individuals (or households) maximize utility subject to a family budget constraint. The budget constraint is a function of wealth, income, available time, health status, and nonlabor income of household members. From the constrained

Figure 6.6 Employment of the Elderly and Migrant Status of Adult Children

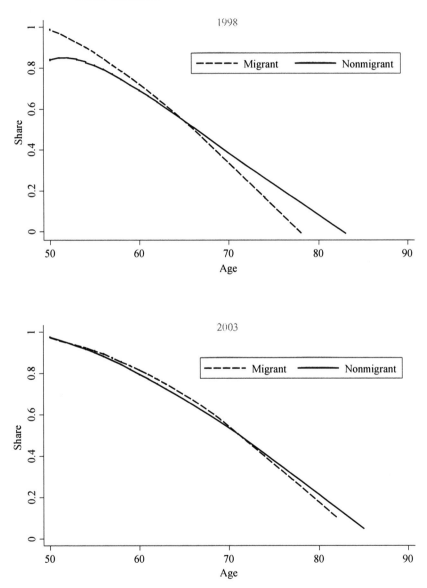

SOURCE: Cai et al. (2012) using survey data from RCRE 2004 Supplemental Rural Household Social Network, Labor Allocation, and Land Use Survey.

Figure 6.6 (continued)

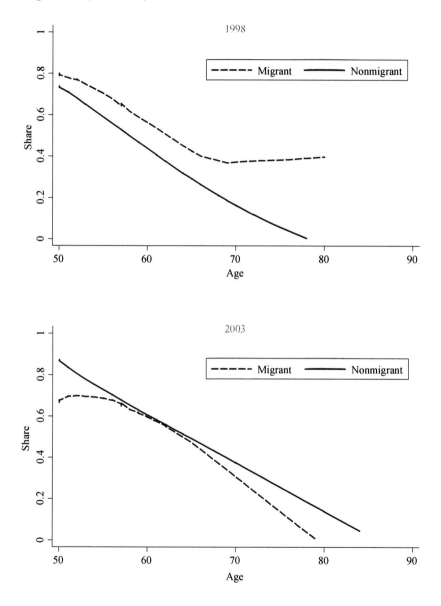

SOURCE: Cai et al. (2012) using survey data from RCRE 2004 Supplemental Rural Household Social Network, Labor Allocation, and Land Use Survey.

utility maximization decision, we conceptualize a general model of labor supply:

$$(6.5) \quad L_{it}^s = f(W_{it}^h, I_{it}^w, I_{it}^{nw}, H_{it}, T_{it}, \mathbf{X}_{it}, V_{it}, \mathbf{D}_{jt}),$$

where labor supply of individual i at time t, L_{it}^s, is a function of household wealth, W_{it}^h, income from work of all household members, I_{it}^w, income unrelated to current work, I_{it}^{nw}, health status, H_{it}, an individual's time endowment, T_{it}, and a vector of individual and household characteristics reflecting preferences, $\mathbf{X}_{it}$, which include own age and demographic characteristics of the household affecting preferences. We also consider the presence of unobserved village institutional characteristics affecting labor supply, V_{it}, and province-year dummy variables controlling for provincewide macroeconomic shocks, $\mathbf{D}_{jt}$. Identifying precise effects of each of these variables can be complicated by three factors that may introduce bias into our estimates: 1) some are imperfectly observed; 2) there are functional relationships among some of these variables (e.g., health status may affect income through productivity, available time, and available household wealth); and 3) labor supply of an elderly individual may be simultaneously determined with the labor supply decisions of other family members. In order to avoid bias in our labor supply models, we use measures of education, age, and health, which are the longer-term determinants of income and wealth.

Because wealth (W_{it}^h) and current labor income (I_{it}^w) of a household are determined by the current and past productivity of household members, we use information on educational attainment and age to characterize productivity. Educational attainment of the elderly themselves is likely to be associated with lifetime earnings and accumulated wealth of the household. We use the average educational attainment of other adult household members to proxy for the value of household labor. Health status also affects productivity and ability to earn income through its impact on capacity for work. Elderly who are ill or suffer physical limitations may be unable to provide much labor for farm activities. Thus, the complete set of proxies for W_{it}^h and I_{it}^w in the reduced form are the educational attainment, health status, age and age-squared of the elderly family member, the average educational attainment of other adults of the household, and numbers of adults in different age categories.

The employment status and location of adult children may have an important impact on the retirement decision. Income earned by the household may be affected by whether a former resident works as a migrant in another location or in a nearby location. In particular, the effect of a migrant child is likely to be ambiguous. On one hand, a migrant adult child may raise household income through increased remittances more than the migrant lowers income through lack of work in agriculture. In this case, we would expect the existence of a migrant son or daughter to be negatively associated with elder parent labor supply. On the other hand, if loss of work capacity when a child migrates is not offset by remittances, migration of an adult child may make it more difficult for an elder parent to retire. Moreover, if residents of a village stand a chance to lose land if it is not kept productive, then land tenure insecurity may create an additional disincentive for retirement. A migrant child will be associated with continued employment of elderly parents if the unobserved risk of land expropriation represented in V_{it} is correlated with factors influencing migration decisions, such as local poverty rates and lack of off-farm opportunities.

Because it includes good measures of elderly health status, we use the China Health and Nutrition Survey to estimate a reduced form labor supply equation:

$$(6.6) \quad L_{it}^s = \beta_1 M_{it} + \beta_2 E_{it}^{own} + \beta_3 E_{it}^{other} + \beta_4 ADL_{it} + \beta_5 Pen_{it} + \mathbf{X}_{it}'\gamma + \mathbf{D}_{jt} + u_{it},$$

where M_{it} is a dummy variable indicating whether a household has a migrant adult child. If increased household income through remittances dominates the effects of lost income from home production and concerns about the risk of lost claim to land, then we would expect the coefficient on M_{it} to be negative.[14] We expect that higher values of educational attainment of elderly, E_{it}^{own}, and other family members, E_{it}^{other}, will be associated with higher wealth and higher potential income and should be negatively related to elderly labor supply. Pension income, Pen_{it}, will be negatively related to labor supply as leisure is generally believed to be a normal good. Finally, we characterize the health of the elderly using z-scores calculated from the average responses to a set of activities of daily living questions, ADL_{it}.[15] We include a vector of individual characteristics, $\mathbf{X}_{it}$, which include age and age-squared and are associated with own productivity, and demographic characteristics of the household, which affect preferences.

In estimating different versions of this model, we find that coefficients on each variable vary with gender, and depend on whether a retirement-age individual is among the young or old elderly. For this reason, we estimate models examining labor supply on subgroups of the population. These include younger men and women between 60 and 70 years of age, and older elderly between 70 and 80 years of age. We also estimate two types of models: binary choice employment models in which the outcome variable is an indicator of whether the elderly household member has engaged in productive income-earning activity over the previous year, and tobit models estimating the number of hours that the individual worked over the year. We present results of key coefficients for employment models in Table 6.5 and impacts on hours in Table 6.6.

Not surprisingly, we find that as potential household incomes increase, the likelihood that an older person is working decreases. This effect is evident in Table 6.5 from examining the effects of pension receipt and educational attainment on employment. For each 1,000 RMB per capita received as pension income, the probability that a man works (whether in his 60s or 70s) falls by 8 percent and the probability that a woman works falls by 6 percent to 6.4 percent. Own educational attainment does not have a significant effect on employment of men in their 60s, but each additional year of education is associated with a 1.6 percent reduction in the probability that a woman in her 60s is employed, and a 1.2–1.3 percent reduction in probability that elderly people in their 70s are working. An increase in the average years of education of other family members has an even stronger depressing effect on labor force participation: higher average levels of education are associated with higher permanent income of the family, and this facilitates retirement.

Ill health, as represented by increases in the activities of daily living (ADL) z-score, also lowers the likelihood that an individual engages in productive activities. Since men are often tasked with more physically demanding jobs in agriculture, it is not surprising that this effect is stronger for men in both age categories than for women. A one standard deviation increase in the ADL z-score is associated with an 11 and 8 percent decrease in probability of employment for men and women,

Table 6.5 Factors Affecting Labor Supply Decisions of the Elderly, Linear Model

Dependent variable: engaged in productive activities during the year

Variable	Ages 60–70		Ages 70–80	
	Men	Women	Men	Women
Has migrant member	0.009	0.058	0.010	0.081***
	(0.041)	(0.046)	(0.046)	(0.032)
Years of education	−0.005	−0.016***	−0.013***	−0.012**
	(0.004)	(0.005)	(0.004)	(0.006)
Years of education of other	−0.017***	−0.020***	−0.018***	−0.015***
household members	(0.005)	(0.005)	(0.005)	(0.004)
ADL z-score	−0.113***	−0.079***	−0.103***	−0.049**
	(0.029)	(0.026)	(0.022)	(0.020)
Income from pension/	−0.083***	−0.064***	−0.084***	−0.060***
1,000 RMB	(0.012)	(0.012)	(0.011)	(0.010)
R-squared	0.237	0.287	0.261	0.179
Observations	483	586	705	818

NOTE: *significant at the 0.10 level; **significant at the 0.05 level; ***significant at the 0.01 level. Migrant family member = a member of the household from a previous round is no longer a household member and has moved outside the home province. All models include age, age-squared, household demographic variables (number of household members over 60, number of children younger than 3, children 3–7, children 8–13, children 14–16, spouse present), and year dummy variables interacted with regions to control for provincewide macroeconomic effects.

SOURCE: China Health and Nutrition Survey (1991, 1993, 1997, 2000, 2004).

respectively, in their 60s, and a 10 and 5 percent decrease for men and women in their 70s.

When we examine the effects of migration on elderly labor supply, we observe positive coefficients for all subgroups. This indicates that the effects of lost farm income and uncertainty about land tenure likely dominate the effects of increased income from remittances in labor supply decisions. Nonetheless, this effect is not statistically significant for men or for women under 70. Women over 70, however, are 8 percent more likely to continue working (most likely in agriculture) if the household has a migrant child.

When we examine the number of hours worked in Table 6.6, we find consistent results. Women over 70 with a migrant child work 411 hours more during a year, or the equivalent of 10 40-hour work weeks. For regions of the country planting two crops a year, this would amount to

Table 6.6 Factors Affecting Hours Worked by the Elderly, Tobit Model

Dependent variable: hours worked

Variable	Ages 60–70		Ages 70–80	
	Men	Women	Men	Women
Has migrant child	44.3	−7.6	199.1	411.2**
	(168.6)	(146.3)	(162.1)	(162.7)
Years of education	15.2	−1.5	−27.0*	−14.3
	(18.3)	(16.1)	(15.1)	(21.5)
Education of other	−12.3	−53.1***	−40.4**	−45.5***
household members	(19.6)	(16.6)	(18.8)	(16.0)
ADL z-score	−416.9***	−299.9***	−294.4***	−211.6***
	(132.7)	(94.8)	(85.1)	(70.6)
Income from	−447.9***	−314.1***	−350.4***	−308.0***
pension/1,000 RMB	(71.1)	(56.7)	(52.9)	(49.0)
Observations	479	586	705	816

NOTE: *significant at the 0.10 level; **significant at the 0.05 level; ***significant at the 0.01 level. Migrant family member = a member of the household from a previous round is no longer a household member and has moved outside the home province.
All models include age, age-squared, household demographic variables (number of household members over 60, number of children younger than 3, children 3–7, children 8–13, children 14–16, spouse present), and year dummy variables interacted with regions to control for provincewide macroeconomic effects.
SOURCE: China Health and Nutrition Survey (1991, 1993, 1997, 2000, 2004).

full-time work during the agricultural busy season. Signs of the effects of education are of the same direction as in the employment models of Table 6.5, but once employed education itself does not have a strong effect on number of hours worked.

Number of hours of labor supplied is also very sensitive to health status and to receipt of pensions. An increase in one standard deviation of the ADL index is associated with a 417-hour reduction in labor supplied by men in their 60s, and a reduction of 350 hours by men in their 70s. Women in their 60s reduce labor supply by 300 hours with a one standard deviation increase in their ADL index, while women in their 70s reduce hours by 211 hours in response to a similar worsening in their health. Pension receipt also has a stronger depressing effect on hours worked by men in their 60s.

The urban elderly are much less likely to work after age 60 than rural elderly, and the results presented here suggest that any mechanism providing the rural elderly with a flow of income in old age is likely to reduce both employment and hours worked. Were China's government to develop a pension system for the rural elderly, it is likely that China's rural residents may choose to retire rather than work until they are no longer able to do so.

CONCLUSION

Whereas the urban elderly receive significant support from pensions, the rural elderly rely primarily on their own labor income and financial support from their children. More men over 60 rely primarily on their own labor income for support, whereas elderly women are somewhat more dependent on transfers from family members. Evidence presented on responsiveness of private transfers to income levels and on the determinants of elderly labor supply suggests that the introduction of a pension system may lead to more security for the elderly without requiring them to continue working into old age.

Private transfers are responsive to low levels of elderly income, but they do not perfectly crowd out income from other sources. At levels of income below the poverty line, transfers from adult children increase as elderly income decreases. When elderly incomes are at and even below the poverty line, however, private transfers are not perfectly crowded out by increases in income. A social welfare benefit that raises incomes of the elderly will not crowd out private transfers.

Migrant children continue to provide remittance support to their parents, but the predicted range of transfers suggests growing risk that low-income elderly may be left in poverty. On average, the predicted transfer from adult children is sufficient to maintain elderly incomes above the poverty line. When the range of potential transfers is considered, however, elderly parents with migrant children clearly face more risk that private transfers will be insufficient to maintain standards of living above the poverty line.

Elderly with higher incomes are less likely to work, as are elderly who are in poor health. Elderly with nonlabor income from pensions or in households with higher levels of education, and thus more income-earning potential, are less likely to participate in income-earning activities. If the elderly receive some type of social welfare support, they are more likely to exit the labor force when over 60.

Elderly in poor health are less likely to work. Declines in health status associated with decreases in ability to perform daily tasks are associated with lower participation in work activity and fewer working hours for those who are still working. Improving the use of the health care system for preventive purposes may keep older workers productive and earning incomes for a longer period of their lives. Further research examining the effects of new rural health insurance programs (under the New Cooperative Medical System) is warranted to determine whether it facilitates improved health and work capacity of older workers.

Migration of adult children may have a significant impact on the work status of elderly women. Having a migrant child in the family raises the probability that a woman over 70 will still be in the labor force and, conditional on working, will work more hours in a year. For men and women under 70, a migrant child has a positive but statistically insignificant effect on participation in income-earning activities.

Notes

The author acknowledges financial support for writing this chapter from two grants provided by the Knowledge for Change Trust Fund at the World Bank (RF-P116739-RESE-TF094568 and RF-P121130-RESE-TF098764).

1. The data were collected before initiation of the national rural pension pilot program in 2009.
2. This finding is consistent with findings in the World Bank's China poverty assessment (Chaudhuri and Datt 2009) using other National Bureau of Statistics data.
3. See World Bank (forthcoming) for a detailed discussion of the evolution of rural *dibao* and other forms of rural social assistance, noting coverage expansion of rural I from just over 8 million in 2005 to almost 48 million in 2009.
4. Using other methods, Cameron and Cobb-Clark (2008) find no evidence that transfers to parents respond to low parent income in Indonesia.
5. Selden (1993) concludes that a transition to the nuclear family imposes a heavy price on the rural elderly. Living arrangements are thought to be important for elderly support across East Asia, including Cambodia (Zimmer and Kim 2002), Thailand (Knodel and Chayovan 1997), and Vietnam (Anh et al. 1997).
6. Two very different conclusions are consistent with evidence of greater incidence of coresidence with age: the oldest, who are more likely to be infirm, tend to move in with adult children; alternatively, if coresidence has an effect on the quality of

care provided, then perhaps only the elderly living with adult children reach old age.

7. Coresidence in rural areas of the four RCRE provinces was also somewhat higher than observed for rural areas of the CHNS panel.

8. Barro (1974), Becker (1974), and Cox (1987) make important theoretical distinctions highlighting different motives for transfers. Much of the empirical research in the United States has suggested that intergenerational intervivos transfers are driven by exchange motives (e.g., Cox and Rank 1992; McGarry 1999) rather than based on altruistic motives. It is important to remember, however, that in the United States, the Social Security safety net provides substantial insurance against poverty in old age, and thus it is not as surprising to find an emphasis on the flow of resources from older to younger generations.

9. We use the 1995 to 2003 waves of RCRE's annual household survey from four provinces (Anhui, Henan, Jiangsu, and Shanxi) in which a supplemental survey (Supplemental Rural Household Social Network, Labor Allocation, and Land Use Survey) was carried out in collaboration with Michigan State University in 2004. A detailed description of the RCRE household survey and comparison to other household surveys conducted in China can be found in Benjamin, Brandt, and Giles (2005).

10. Other regressors included among the X's are age, years of schooling, marital status, an indicator for whether the household has any members in schooling, the number of household residents, the number of working household residents, shares of household residents in different demographic categories, numbers of nonresident family members in different demographic categories, village dummy variables to control for the local economic environment, and province-year dummies to control for macroeconomic shocks.

11. Specifically, we use a bandwidth of 0.25 with observations weighted using a tricube weighting function as calculated by the lowess command in Stata. The lowess estimator was developed by Cleveland (1979) and has a benefit over some kernel estimators in that it does not suffer from bias near the end points.

12. The Poverty Assessment (Chaudhuri and Datt 2009) emphasized that 65 percent of rural migrants had lived in the current city where they were working for more than three years, and this duration was significantly longer than reported in a similar survey conducted in 2001.

13. The information comes from a retrospective work history carried out as part of a supplemental survey conducted with RCRE in 2004. The supplemental survey asked about the work history of current and former household residents and their parents.

14. It is also important to remember that we do not identify a causal relationship between migrant children and elderly labor supply. Unobservable factors related to the family (related to motivation, interest in income, or specific abilities) may affect both the migration decisions of adult children and labor supply decisions of their parents.

15. Bound (1991) has argued that information from ADLs contributes less bias than self-reported health in models of retirement behavior. In the CHNS, individuals

over age 50 are asked to rate the difficulty from 1 (no difficulty) to 4 (cannot do at all) of the following activities: walking a kilometer; sitting continuously for two hours; standing up after sitting for a long time; climbing one staircase; lifting or raising a 5-kilogram bag; squatting down, kneeling down, or bending over; bathing yourself; eating by yourself; putting on your clothes; using the toilet. We calculate average responses to these questions for each individual, and then calculate z-scores over all elderly.

References

Anh, Truong, Bui T. Cuong, Daniel Goodkind, and John Knodel. 1997. "Living Arrangements, Patrilinearity and Sources of Support among Elderly Vietnamese." *Asia-Pacific Population Journal* 12(4): 69–88.

Barro, Robert J. 1974. "Are Government Bonds Net Wealth?" *Journal of Political Economy* 82(6): 1095–1117.

Becker, Gary. 1974. "A Theory of Social Interactions." *Journal of Political Economy* 82(6): 1063–1093.

Benjamin, Dwayne, Loren Brandt, and Jia-Zhueng Fan. 2003. "Ceaseless Toil? Health and Labor Supply of the Elderly in Rural China." William Davidson Institute Working Paper No. 579, Department of Economics. Toronto: University of Toronto.

Benjamin, Dwayne, Loren Brandt, and John Giles. 2005. "The Evolution of Income Inequality in Rural China." *Economic Development and Cultural Change* 53(4): 769–824.

Benjamin, Dwayne, Loren Brandt, John Giles, and Sangui Wang. 2008. "Income Inequality during China's Economic Transition." In *China's Great Economic Transformation*, Loren Brandt and Thomas Rawski, eds. New York: Cambridge University Press, 729–775.

Benjamin, Dwayne, Loren Brandt, and Scott Rozelle. 2000. "Aging, Well-Being, and Social Security in Rural North China." *Population and Development Review, Supplement* 26: 89–116.

Bound, John. 1991. "Self-Reported versus Objective Measures of Health in Retirement Models." *Journal of Human Resources* 26(1): 106–138.

Cai, Fang, John Giles, and Xin Meng. 2006. "How Well Do Children Insure Parents against Low Retirement Income? An Analysis Using Survey Data from Urban China." *Journal of Public Economics* 90(12): 2229–2255.

Cai, Fang, John Giles, Philip O'Keefe, and Dewen Wang. 2012. *The Elderly and Old Age Support in Rural China: Challenges and Prospects*. Washington, DC: World Bank.

Cameron, Lisa Ann, and Deborah A. Cobb-Clark. 2008. "Do Co-Residency and Financial Transfers from Children Reduce the Need for Elderly Parents to Work in Developing Countries?" *Journal of Population Economics* 21(4): 1007–1033.

China Health and Nutrition Survey. Various years. China Center for Disease Control and Prevention and the Carolina Population Center. Chapel Hill, NC: University of North Carolina at Chapel Hill. http://www.cpc.unc.edu/ projects/china (accessed January 16, 2012).

Chaudhuri, Shubham, and Gaurav Datt. 2009. *From Poor Areas to Poor People: China's Evolving Poverty Agenda, an Assessment of Poverty and Inequality in China.* Washington, DC: World Bank.

Cleveland, W.S. 1979. "Robust Locally Weighted Regression and Smoothing Scatterplots." *Journal of American Statistical Association* 74(368): 829–836.

Cox, Donald. 1987. "Motives for Private Income Transfers." *Journal of Political Economy* 95(3): 509–546.

Cox, Donald, Bruce E. Hansen, and Emmanuel Jimenez. 2004. "How Responsive to Private Transfers to Income? Evidence from a Laissez-Faire Economy." *Journal of Public Economics* 88(9–10): 2193–2219.

Cox, Donald, and Mark R. Rank. 1992. "Inter-Vivos Transfers and Intergenerational Exchange." *Review of Economics and Statistics* 74(2): 305–314.

Duclos, Jean-Yves, Abdelkrim Araar, and John Giles. 2010. "Chronic and Transient Poverty: Measurement and Estimation, with Evidence from China." *Journal of Development Economics* 91(2): 266–277.

Giles, John. 2006. "Is Life More Risky in the Open? Household Risk-Coping and the Opening of China's Labor Markets." *Journal of Development Economics* 81(1): 25–60.

Giles, John, and Ren Mu. 2007. "Elderly Parent Health and the Migration Decision of Adult Children: Evidence from Rural China." *Demography* 44(2): 265–288.

Giles, John, Dewen Wang, and Changbao Zhao. 2010. "Can China's Rural Elderly Count on Support from Adult Children? Implications of Rural-to-Urban Migration." *Journal of Population Ageing* 3(3–4): 183–204.

Jalan, Jyotsna, and Martin Ravallion. 1999. "Are the Poor Less Well Insured? Evidence on Vulnerability to Income Risk in Rural China." *Journal of Development Economics* 58(1): 61–82.

———. 2002. "Geographic Poverty Traps? A Micro Model of Consumption Growth in Rural China." *Journal of Applied Econometrics* 17(4): 329–346.

Jiang, Chen, and Xiaojun Zhao. 2009. "A Study on the Opportunity Cost of China's Elderly Care." *Management World* [Guanli Shijie] 10: 80–87.

Kanbur, Ravi, and Xiaobo Zhang. 1999. "Which Regional Inequality? The Evolution of Rural-Urban and Inland-Coastal Inequality in China from 1983 to 1995." *Journal of Comparative Economics* 27: 686–701.

————. 2005. "Fifty Years of Regional Inequality in China: A Journey through Central Planning, Reform, and Openness." *Review of Development Economics* 9(1): 87–106.

Knodel, John, and Napaporn Chayovan. 1997. "Family Support and Living Arrangements of Thai Elderly." *Asia-Pacific Population Journal* 12(4): 51–68.

Lee, Yean-Ju, and Zhenyu Xiao. 1998. "Children's Support for Elderly Parents in Urban and Rural China: Results from a National Survey." *Journal of Cross-Cultural Gerontology* 13(1): 39–62.

Li, Shuzhuo, Song Lu, and Marcus W. Feldman. 2009. "Intergenerational Support and Subjective Health of Older People in Rural China: A Gender-Based Longitudinal Study." *Australasian Journal on Ageing* 28(2): 81–86.

Marriage Law. 2001. The Marriage Law of the People's Republic of China, Section 3, Article 21. http://www.nyconsulate.prchina.org/eng/lsqz/laws/t42222.htm (accessed July 2, 2012).

McGarry, Kathleen. 1999. "Inter-Vivos Transfers and Intended Bequests." *Journal of Public Economics* 73(3): 321–325.

NBS (National Bureau of Statistics). 2006. *2005 One Percent Population Sample Data.* Beijing: China Statistics Press.

Pang, Lihua, Alan de Brauw, and Scott Rozelle. 2004. "Working until You Drop: The Elderly of Rural China." *China Journal* 52: 73–96.

Ravallion, Martin, and Shaohua Chen. 2007. "China's (Uneven) Progress against Poverty." *Journal of Development Economics* 82(1) (January 2007): 1–42.

Research Center for Rural Economy (RCRE). Various years. Rural Household Surveys for 1993–2003 from Anhui, Henan, Jiangsu, and Shanxi Provinces. Beijing: Ministry of Agriculture, Research Center for Rural Economy.

————. 2004. Supplemental Rural Household Social Network, Labor Allocation, and Land Use Survey. Beijing: Ministry of Agriculture, Research Center for Rural Economy.

Selden, Mark. 1993. "Family Strategies and Structures in Rural North China." In *Chinese Families in the Post-Mao Era*, Deborah Davis and Stevan Harrell, eds. Berkeley: University of California Press, pp. 139–164.

World Bank. Forthcoming. *Social Assistance in Rural China: Tackling Poverty through Rural Dibao.* Washington, DC: World Bank.

Yao, Yingmei. 2006. "Issues of Old Age Support for the 'Empty Nest' Rural Elderly in Developed Region, a Case of Rural Zhejiang Province." *Population Research* [Renkou Yanjiu] 30(6): 38–46.

Yatchew, Adonis. 2003. *Semiparametric Regression for the Applied Econometrician.* New York: Cambridge University Press.

Zimmer, Zachary, and Sovan Kiry Kim. 2002. "Living Arrangements and

Socio-Demographic Conditions of Older Adults in Cambodia." Policy Research Division Working Paper No. 157. New York: Population Council.

Zimmer, Zachary, and Julia Kwong. 2003. "Family Size and Support of Older Adults in Urban and Rural China: Current Effects and Future Implications." *Demography* 40(1): 23–44.

7
China in 2049

Zhiwu Chen
Yale School of Management

The People's Republic of China was founded in 1949, and its current economic reforms were implemented beginning in 1978 following the end of the Cultural Revolution. Since then, China has become an economic powerhouse, neatly timing the advent of globalization and organized free trade.

The purpose of this chapter is to examine historical trends in, and the impact of, modern reforms on the Chinese economy; to look at what is likely to happen to growth, earnings, and savings over the next four decades; and to compare the Chinese economy to the U.S. economy over this period of time.

THE BIG PICTURE

Figure 7.1 shows a likely growth pattern of the Chinese economy in the coming decades. It depicts three different phases. The initial phase goes from 2010 to 2016, during which no major shifts in the growth model of the Chinese economy will likely occur. Growth continues at a rate of about 8.5 percent per year despite the likelihood that the Chinese government will implement substantial changes in policies relating to investments, exports, and domestic consumption that could impact growth. Although there is much talk in the Chinese media about how reforms in these sectors will have a negative effect, it is unlikely such reforms will have much negative impact due to political reasons and other complications.

It is presumed that, in 2016, there will be a peak of the Chinese economy in the real term followed by a downturn—the second phase—of 12 percent in the year 2017. Why a 12 percent decline? This predic-

Figure 7.1 Possible Future Path for the United States and China

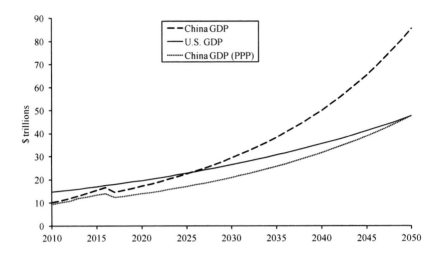

NOTE: Assumptions: China's GDP grows at 8.5 percent until 2016, declines by 12 percent in 2017, and then at 5.5 percent a year thereafter; U.S. grows at 3 percent a year.

tion is inferred from the Asian financial crisis that occurred in 1998. There are many similarities between the current Chinese economy and the Korean economy during that period. As shown in Figure 7.2, per capita GDP in Korea rose sharply during the first half of the 1990s only to drop precipitously beginning in 1997. I assume a similar pattern will occur in the Chinese economy.

However, it should be noted that other organizations predict continued, steady growth during this period. For instance, the Conference Board (2012) projects growth at 8.0 percent in 2012, 6.0 percent annually in 2013–2016, and 3.5 percent annually in 2017–2025.

After the setback in 2017, the Chinese economy should resume its growth—the third phase. When this occurs, beginning in 2017–2018, the growth rate should be 5–6 percent per year through 2049. The International Monetary Fund (IMF) projects average annual growth of 5.56 percent for years 2009–2050 (Dadush and Stancil 2009). During this same period, some analysts predict that the U.S. economy would grow at 3 percent per year, which is possibly an optimistic prediction considering its unsteady growth rate in recent years. The IMF projects an annual growth rate for the United States of 2.7 percent over the same period.

The resumption of growth should occur due to socially and politically acceptable reforms that commonly take place in any economy, including the U.S. economy and the economies of other advanced nations, when hit by crisis. In fact, a looming economic crisis is partly what spurred the reformers led by Deng Xiaoping to undertake major political and economic reforms in 1978 just after the Mao-era Cultural Revolution, during which many people were displaced or lost their lives or property for proposing political and economic changes. Without Deng's reforms, the Chinese economy and society overall would not have evolved to what it is today.

Even now, China's economy is heavily influenced by its major policymakers. Fundamentally, there should be incentives for major political, economic, and cultural changes to a society. From 1979 to 2009, China's leaders were prompted to implement reforms in these

Figure 7.2 GDP per Capita for Korea, 1990–2000 (current $)

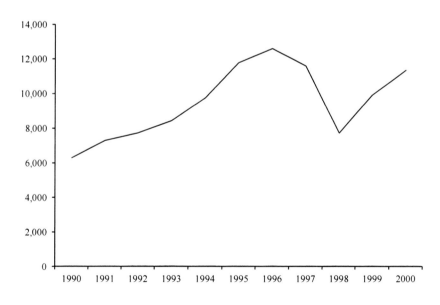

SOURCE: EconStats (2012).

areas in order to maintain strong and continued economic growth, and I predict they will continue this process even after 2017–2018.

As seen in Figure 7.1, in 2049, China's nominal GDP should surpass the United States' nominal GDP, under the *ceteris paribus* assumption that the RMB-dollar exchange rate remains relatively stable over time. If purchasing power parity (PPP) is taken into account, China's GDP is projected to surpass the United States' GDP in 2027, about 22 years earlier than in the nominal term.

HISTORICAL PERSPECTIVE

Let us take a historical look at the Chinese economy using Figure 7.3. The per capita GDP of China up until 1950 was almost stagnant and remained around $500 per annum. From 1950 to 1973, the GDP per capita per annum increased about 60 percent, and from 1973 to 1998 it increased by about 300 percent. Furthermore, it continued to grow so

Figure 7.3 China's per Capita GDP over 2000 Years

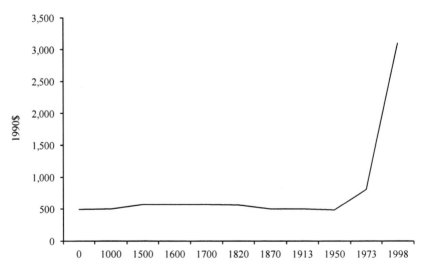

SOURCE: Maddison (2001).

that the GDP per capita in 2011 is estimated at $5,184 (IMF 2011). In short, as shown in Figure 7.3, most of the growth in China's per capita GDP occurred in the last 30 to 60 years.

Figure 7.4 provides a more detailed look at the rapid growth in per capita GDP that occurred recently using PPP-adjusted dollars. Using this measure, the figure shows that per capita GDP increased by a factor of 20 times over the period 1980–2009.

Observing income growth and productivity growth together helps provide a more complete picture of China's long-term economic progress. Here I focus on the income side, and for comparison I provide a measure for how much in terms of consumables a laborer earns for a day's labor.

Figure 7.5 provides a timeline showing real earnings in terms of meat and rice. In 1769, a day's labor earned a typical worker about 3 jins (China's unit of weight measurement as equivalent to pounds) of meat; in 1850 it was around 2 pounds. From then until 1973 a day's labor

Figure 7.4 China's Past Growth in per Capita GDP (in PPP-adjusted $)

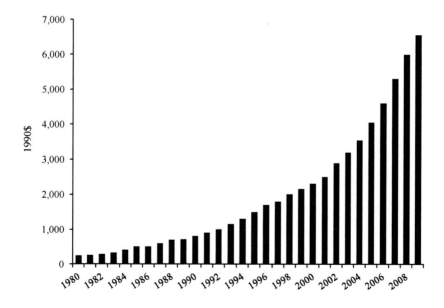

SOURCE: CIA (2010).

earned less than 2 jins. Currently, a typical Chinese laborer earns the equivalent of about 10 jins of meat per day, which implies that workers today are about 4 times as productive as the workers before 1973, even taking into consideration the rising prices. Rice as a measure followed a similar path, but beginning in 1973, the productivity increase is even greater, almost 10 times that before 1973.

What has caused such growth and progress in China? Many economists and commentators say it is due to the vast amount of cheap labor available in China. But, in fact, China's population has been declining as the share of the global population. In 1830, China had about 40 percent of the world's population. In 1913, China's population was one-third of the world's population. China now has roughly 1.4 billion

Figure 7.5 Real Earnings per Day for a Beijing Worker

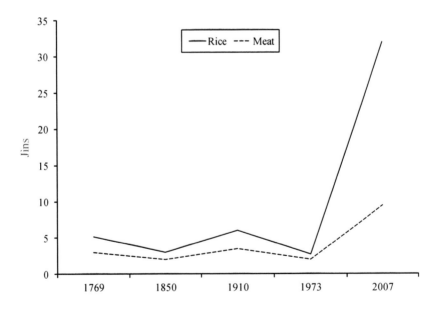

NOTE: This figure is based on the assumption that the daily earning in 1769 was 77 Tongchien (copper dollar, currency unit in Qing Dynasty); in 1973 $1 Chinese Yuan (Chinese dollar, Renminbi): and nowadays $50 Chinese Yuan.

SOURCE: Various sources. The price indices in Qing Dynasty come from the files of Holland East Indian Company.

people, or about 20 percent of the global population. So the argument that China's vast and low-cost workforce is the main driving force of economic growth is well grounded. If such a labor force was available in the past, why didn't China experience growth earlier on? In addition, in 2011 the minimum wage in China was raised in most of the country by 21.7 percent, making China's labor force higher paid than several of its East Asian neighbors (BBC 2011). What is it, then, that propels such dynamic economic growth in China?

To understand the driving factor of economic growth of present-day China, let's consider a quote from a book published in Shanghai in 1914, *Finance in China* (Wagel 1914). The following excerpt, quoted then in the *New York Times*, highlighted the threat of China's economy to Western economies:

> It is often said that the peril of today is not the Chinese behind the gun, but the Chinese as the manufacturers of guns and of many other things, equally calling for the highest technical skill. It has been the fashion of newspaper writers dealing with the development of China to state that the danger to the West lies in the industrial expansion of China, and it is averred that the Chinese, with their cheap labour and keen aptitude for imitation, competing with the dear labour and the heavy cost of transportation of the West, would certainly be able to beat the latter. (Wagel 1914, p. 291)

After the publication of Wagel's book, Western nations became nervous about China's rise because they thought that China would inevitably become economically dominant due to, as Wagel points out, its cheap labor relative to the West. However, such anxieties were sometimes seen as contributing factors that helped foment the Cultural Revolution, war, and other disruptions in China.

In what way is China different now from its past? Figure 7.6 shows the correlation between GDP growth and the population of China over several centuries to 2008.

Going back to 1600, the correlation between population and GDP growth was almost 100 percent. By 1820, the correlation remained very high, almost 97 percent. These high correlations were due to the fact that labor was the primary, if not the sole, factor of production. During that period, modern technology was practically nonexistent, production was almost exclusively labor intensive, therefore GDP grew in step with the population. It wasn't until the effects of the industrial revolution spread

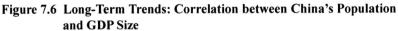

Figure 7.6 Long-Term Trends: Correlation between China's Population and GDP Size

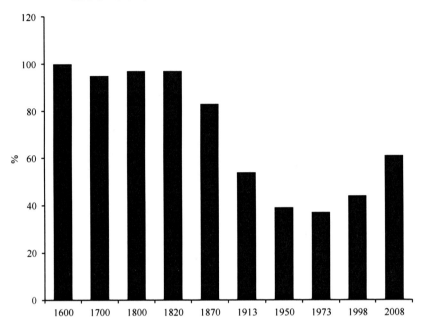

SOURCE: Maddison (2001).

to China in the latter part of the nineteenth century that the correlation declined. Production became more capital intensive, and hence the correlation between population and GDP declined. This decrease continued until after 1950 when it began to increase. The correlation grew more quickly beginning around 1973 as China began to take advantage of the trend of globalization and a freer trade environment.

Globalization opened up more of the Chinese economy to international markets mainly due to the establishment of the World Trade Organization (WTO), whose policies tend to benefit China more than other economies. This international order of trade that has been encouraged by Western industrialized economies is a key reason for China's economic success during the past 30 years.

In the seventeenth, eighteenth, and nineteenth centuries, the international order was based on a country's military power, which implied a gunboat-based order rather than a rule-based order. The East India Company of the eighteenth century is an example of a successful practitioner of gunboat-based order. It maintained its own navy and military power, facilitating its participation in international trade. Eventually, technology developed during the industrial revolution in the Western nations spread to China, enabling it to transition from a gunboat-based economy to a rule-based economy. Today, rule-based order provides the basis for the entry of multinational corporations in China such as General Electric, whose army of lawyers help it conduct business.

Gunboat-based and rule-based trade and investment have vast differences in transaction costs. For instance, employing lawyers is less expensive than maintaining a military force. Therefore, the transaction costs for trade today are less than during the gunboat-based age. This allows China to incur much lower transaction costs for trade today and serves as another reason why its economy is less encumbered and freer to grow.

Let's compare the reforms under Deng Xiaoping in 1978 with those made in the nineteenth century under the Qing Dynasty (1644–1911). During the Qing Dynasty, Li Hongzhang, a leading statesman, built military power that allowed China to become economically competitive. Without this power China would not have been able to engage, on a significant scale, in international trade and investment. On the other hand, Deng Xiaoping did not have to build military power to compete for trade. Instead he implemented market-oriented rules and regulations that attracted foreign direct investment and international trade.

Figure 7.7 shows the per capita GDP of China and the rest of the world from over 2000 years ago until the end of the twentieth century. As depicted by the steep slope of the line, China began gaining on the rest of the world after 1973, when globalization and the reforms implemented five years later began to have an impact.

As Wagel (1914) pointed out, China is sometimes characterized as having a keen ability to imitate new technologies that were developed by others, and the gains China has made since 1973 are due to such imitation. However, there are both pros and cons to this depiction. It is an advantage when countries only need to imitate in order to be able to pursue fast growth. However, such growth can also impede incentives to innovate and to conduct timely institutional reforms, so imitation can also be seen as a disadvantage.

Figure 7.7 Per Capita GDP: World vs. China

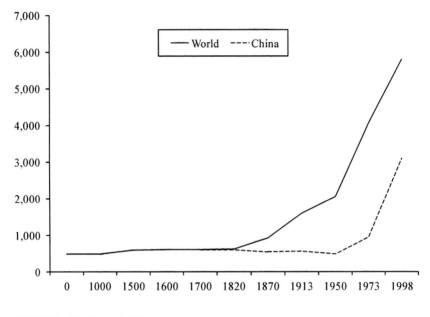

SOURCE: Maddison (2001).

Cost-saving manufacturing technologies developed in the twentieth century spread throughout the world in part due to policies implemented by the WTO. China became the major benefactor of this dis-
persal of technology. Still, there is another factor that helps to explain
the success of China's economy in the last 30 years: the change in
policies that affect the decision making on resource allocation and its
control. China's economic policies are formulated in such a way that
they are conducive to fast economic growth despite the fact that there
are some negative side-effects that resulted, such as the dominance of
state-owned enterprises (SOEs) in certain industries, environmental
degradation, crowding-out of private property to the public sector, and
substandard working conditions.

The rising pace of factor productivity growth can be attributed in
part to overinvestment and the emergence of excess capacity in a number of important industries. China emerged as the world's largest steel
producer in 1996 when its output reached 100 million metric tons, put-

ting it ahead of both the United States and Japan for the first time. The industry has continued to grow at a rapid pace. This is an example of the extent of China's industrialization and serves as just one example of an SOE that contributes substantially to the growth of its economy.

World Trade Organization membership had an immediate impact on Chinese economic growth, paving the way for more efficient day-to-day operations of Chinese corporations while reducing the risk premium investors applied to investment in the country. In addition, WTO membership established a powerful catalyst for a more serious approach to economic reform and industrial efficiency. As the benefits of those changes materialized, China achieved sustainable incremental economic growth while gradually reducing the risk premium of investment. This significantly cut the discount at which Chinese equities have traded against global market peers. As a major force driving the national economy of China, the fast expansion of SOEs has contributed significantly to China becoming the world's second-largest economy.

OWNERSHIP STRUCTURE OF PRODUCTIVE ASSETS

At the end of 2006, according to government records, land owned by the government was valued at 50 trillion RMB. At the same time, there were about 119,000 SOEs valued at about 29 trillion RMB. Therefore, the combined value of government land ownership plus SOEs amounted to 79 trillion RMB, which was roughly one-tenth of comparable U.S. government holdings. A few years later these values grew due to the expanding economy and land value appreciation. While at the end of 2006 state-owned assets were roughly 76 percent of the total national wealth in China, in 2010 that percentage likely declined to roughly 70 percent of the total national wealth because of the increasing trend toward privatization, particularly in the industrial sector.

Figure 7.8 shows a comparison of total government expenditures with total household expenditures in China as a percentage of GDP. In 1952, household consumption was about 69 percent of GDP, pretty close to today's household expenditures in the United States, which is roughly 71 percent of GDP. At the founding of the People's Republic of China, the economy was driven by household consumption. Over the

**Figure 7.8 China's Household Consumption vs. Government
Expenditure as a Percentage of GDP**

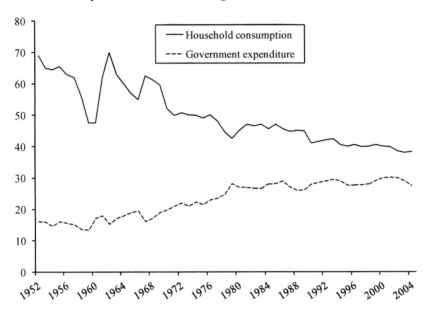

SOURCE: Various sources.

years, during the planned economy period, this consumption declined
so that now it is roughly 36 percent of GDP. Even in the reform period
this share continues to decline. On the other hand, government expenditure as a percentage of GDP increased from 16 percent in 1952 to about
30 percent in the 2000s. Government expenditures as a share of GDP
have almost doubled in the last 60 years, while private consumption
expenditure as a percentage of GDP declined.

The government in China also has practically unchecked taxation
power. To introduce a new tax or to raise tax rates, the government
doesn't have to go through parliamentary debates. The ministry of
finance and state council generally meet together and make new tax
policy. It is somewhat daunting that a few people could simply gather
in a room at the time of their choosing and make decisions that may
alter the tax rates and policies of the world's second-largest economy.
There is no accountability to the taxpayers. As a result, government

expenditures as the share of GDP, as the bold line depicts in the figure, trend upward.

The Chinese government's budget was roughly 8 trillion RMB in 2010, which is about half of the U.S. annual government budget at the current exchange rate. But, if we use PPP, the Chinese budget may actually be bigger than the U.S. budget. The main question facing China's policymakers is how to spend that 8 trillion RMB. Social groups and political leaders are both influential in this decision. In China the political situation influences the distribution of resources, including how the budget is apportioned to different provinces and societies. Public accountability of the government budget spending is still waiting on establishment of the democratic institutions in China.

The growing concern among those tracking China's economy comes from the fact that SOEs, which were previously focused on manufacturing industries, are entering the financial industry, thereby expanding their influence further into the economy. They are doing so for two reasons: 1) it is useful for satisfying their own development needs and assures that they receive the financial support they need to grow, and 2) some SOEs see value in having a financial license or room for financial equity growth, and thus hope to profit from undertakings in finance. However, I believe that these two points, taken either individually or together, are not sufficient reasons to justify allowing SOEs' expansion into the financial domain.

SAVING

It is true that Chinese people generally save more of their income than people of other nationalities. As Figure 7.9 shows, the gross savings rate as a percentage of GDP rose from around 40 percent in 1992 to about 50 percent in 2006. However, looking at just the household sector's savings as a percentage of GDP, there is little variation over that period of time, staying at about 20 percent, although trending slightly upward in the 2000s. This relatively steady rate is due mainly to the fall in the share of household income as a share of national income rather than a decline in the household savings rate (Prasad 2009).

**Figure 7.9   Household, Enterprise, and Government Savings as a
Percentage of GDP, China, 1992–2006**

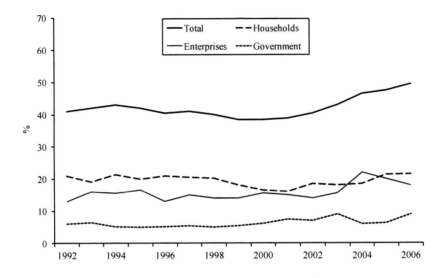

SOURCE: China Statistical Yearbook (1995–2009). Flow of Funds Accounts.

Savings by SOEs has been more evident. Beginning in 2003, SOEs'
savings rate as a percentage of GDP jumped sharply from about 15 percent to over 20 percent before falling back slightly. The SOEs are not
subject to monitoring by the National People's Congress or other governmental agencies, and they are not required to redistribute profits or
remit them to the Ministry of Finance. Their profits and increased value
are not translated into consumption since households do not receive
these benefits. The same is true for the sales of land and SOEs themselves, the proceeds of which go to the government treasury. Government saving also increased gradually to about 9 percent from a steady 5
percent seen throughout the 1990s.

Figure 7.10 shows gross savings as a percentage of GDP in seven
other industrialized nations—including the United States—and the
world overall. Note that, over the same period of 1992–2006, the rate
ranges from a low of 13.3 percent (in Canada in 1992) to a high of 33.8
percent (in Japan, also in 1992). The U.S. rate ranges from a low of
14.4 percent in 1993 to a high of 18.8 percent in 1998 (EconStats 2012).

**Figure 7.10 Gross Savings as a Percentage of GDP, Seven Countries plus
the World, 1992–2006**

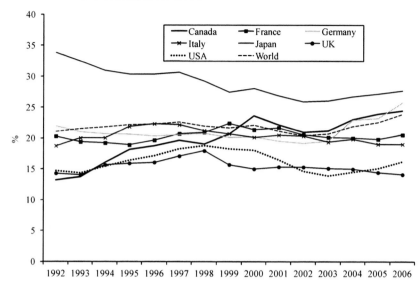

SOURCE: EconStats (2012).

Therefore, it is apparent that China's gross savings rate is quite high relative to other large nations, which is one reason why its policymakers are encouraging domestic consumption, which has not been growing as fast as GDP, as a means of rebalancing the nation's growth and reducing its account surplus.

SUMMARY

China's economy is mainly investment and export driven as opposed to being driven by domestic consumption like the U.S. economy is. Because of that, the consequences are that the economy is too dependent on these sectors. It also finds itself overly dependent on energy-intensive industries and insufficiently so on the service sector. Transitioning to a more balanced economy, one in which private consumption plays a greater role, will be a challenge for China's economic policy-makers. Because of the political pressure applied by the vested interest group who benefit from the current policies, there is no incentive for them to alter policy in order to transition to a more balanced economy. Other problematic consequences resulting from how China's economy has developed include the crowding out of private firms in industries in which SOEs became dominant players and barriers to legal development and the rule of law in the economy.

Still, the current model for economic growth in China will likely continue despite recessions and other economic uncertainty worldwide. In fact, these issues emphasize the importance of a highly coordinated state-controlled economy, particularly the rising influence of SOEs through state-owned banks and other financial institutions.

To summarize, the economic benefits accrued as a result of the industrial revolution have been completely absorbed into China's economy, as have the benefits from the international movement of investment and capital. China's current growth may be attributed mainly to government sector involvements in the economy. Risks remain, however. These include being overly reliant on the government-dominated economic model, the ascending SOEs and the power they continue to amass, an increasingly tougher environment for private and foreign firms to operate freely in, and the fact that local governments are becoming major borrowers from banks.

References

BBC. 2011. "China Minimum Wage Up by 21.7% despite Economic Cooling." London: BBC. http://www.bbc.co.uk/news/business-15456509 (accessed January 31, 2012).

Central Intelligence Agency (CIA). 2010. *The World Factbook*. New York: Skyhorse Publishing.

Conference Board. 2012. The Conference Board Global Economic Outlook. New York: The Conference Board. http://www.conference-board.org/data/globaloutlook.cfm (accessed February 6, 2012).

Dadush, Uri, and Bennett Stancil. 2009. "The G20 in 2050." *International Economic Bulletin*. November 19. http://carnegieendowment.org/2009/11/19/g20-in-2050/cv (accessed February 6, 2012).

EconStats. 2012. World Economic Outlook (WEO) Data. Washington, DC:

International Monetary Fund. http://www.econstats.com/weo/vol5.htm (accessed February 1, 2012).

IMF. 2011. World Economic Outlook Database. Washington, DC: International Monetary Fund. http://www.imf.org/external/pubs/ft/weo/2011/02/weodata/index.aspx (accessed February 2, 2012).

Maddison, Angus. 2001. *The World Economy: A Millennial Perspective*. Paris: Organisation for Economic Co-Operation and Development.

Prasad, Eswar. 2009. "Rebalancing Growth in Asia." NBER Working Paper No. 15169. Cambridge, MA: National Bureau of Economic Research.

Wagel, Srinivas R. 1914. *Finance in China*. Shanghai: North-China Daily News and Herald, Ltd.

Authors

Gene H. Chang is a professor of economics and the director of the Asian Studies Institute at the University of Toledo.

Zhiwu Chen is a professor of finance at Yale University.

Mary Gallagher is an associate professor of political science at the University of Michigan.

John Giles is a senior labor economist in the Development Research Group at the World Bank and a research fellow at the Institute for Labor (IZA) in Bonn.

Wei-Chiao Huang is a professor of economics at Western Michigan University.

Robert B. Koopman is the chief economist at the United States International Trade Commission.

Terry Sicular is a professor of economics at Western University, Canada.

Huizhong Zhou is a professor of economics at Western Michigan University.

Index

The italic letters *f*, *n*, and *t* following a page number indicate that the subject information of the entry heading is within a figure, note, or table, respectively, on that page. Double italics indicate multiple but consecutive elements.

About the Institute

The W.E. Upjohn Institute for Employment Research is a nonprofit research organization devoted to finding and promoting solutions to employment-related problems at the national, state, and local levels. It is an activity of the W.E. Upjohn Unemployment Trustee Corporation, which was established in 1932 to administer a fund set aside by Dr. W.E. Upjohn, founder of The Upjohn Company, to seek ways to counteract the loss of employment income during economic downturns.

The Institute is funded largely by income from the W.E. Upjohn Unemployment Trust, supplemented by outside grants, contracts, and sales of publications. Activities of the Institute comprise the following elements: 1) a research program conducted by a resident staff of professional social scientists; 2) a competitive grant program, which expands and complements the internal research program by providing financial support to researchers outside the Institute; 3) a publications program, which provides the major vehicle for disseminating the research of staff and grantees, as well as other selected works in the field; and 4) an Employment Management Services division, which manages most of the publicly funded employment and training programs in the local area.

The broad objectives of the Institute's research, grant, and publication programs are to 1) promote scholarship and experimentation on issues of public and private employment and unemployment policy, and 2) make knowledge and scholarship relevant and useful to policymakers in their pursuit of solutions to employment and unemployment problems.

Current areas of concentration for these programs include causes, consequences, and measures to alleviate unemployment; social insurance and income maintenance programs; compensation; workforce quality; work arrangements; family labor issues; labor-management relations; and regional economic development and local labor markets.

CPSIA information can be obtained at www.ICGtesting.com
Printed in the USA
BVOW08s1355020813

327652BV00007B/24/P